NORTH AYRSHIRE

D0190347

Vanilla Black

———

NORTH AYRSHIRE LIBRARIES	
06973345	
Bertrams	15/05/2015
641.563	£25.00
B	

ANDREW DARGUE

WITH ALICE HANSEN

Vanilla Black

―――――

FRESH FLAVOURS FOR
YOUR VEGETARIAN KITCHEN

PHOTOGRAPHS BY
EMMA LEE

Contents

The Food

This book is from the people behind Vanilla Black, but the food is not from the restaurant. Well, not entirely, anyway. The recipes here will give an insight into some of the things that we do, but this is a book for home cooks.

At our restaurant, we serve a twist on traditional English and French classical dishes, reinvented as vegetarian food. The fact that it is vegetarian is not the point; in fact, it's neither here nor there. It's not food for vegetarians, in the same way that an Italian restaurant does not serve food for Italian people alone. Ours is just good food done in the modern style, and done well. This book is for all people who are interested in food. Modern food.

The dishes we cook at the restaurant are forward-thinking. Yes, we use dehydrators to take every drop of moisture out of a tarragon sponge to render it crisp. And we are also guilty of sous-vide-ing the odd item or two. And it's true that – as in most restaurants – we have a couple of guys washing up constantly. We are guessing that, unless you're astoundingly lucky, you do not have the pair of them in your kitchen.

So, in this book, we give Vanilla Black recipes adapted for the home kitchen. They are still interesting, with flavours, textures and methods that will challenge you both as a cook and as an eater. Our food is challenging. It's different. Smashing stereotypes and proving that vegetarian cuisine can become mainstream is the reason this book you are holding exists.

The recipes here are both intriguing and delicious. We infuse oil with chives to make mayonnaise. We toast oats before cooking, to make porridge taste nutty. We take butter to the point of caramelisation before using it in a brown butter filling for old-style pineapple upside-down cake. Within these pages, there's a recipe for a new and improved cheese-and-onion pasty and chutneys and jams (and brown sauce) made in the microwave. We make home-made curds. We pickle grapes. When Savoy cabbage pudding was on the menu, we couldn't make enough of them. People used to order them when they rang to book. It is made from only cabbage, cheese, butter and stale bread, but they work together astoundingly well. And there are also trickier techniques here, such as roasting white chocolate to serve with a cutting-edge dessert. This book is about cooking something simple or something technical, but above all it is about having fun and trying flavour combinations you may not have previously considered.

Many times a day in the restaurant we hear 'I'm not vegetarian, but that was really good.' You don't have to be vegetarian. Just try this food. Play with it. See what you think. And if you want to serve it with a piece of grilled chicken, be our guest.

However you serve it, enjoy it.

Us

'Apologies in advance, no pasta bake or vegetable curry.' Ten years ago we didn't think we would have to put that warning on our website, but we did.

We became vegetarian for no major reason. No dreadlocks were involved. We didn't hug trees. We kept our leather settee. We just stopped eating meat and fish. If someone had told us at 16 that we would be vegetarian adults, we would have laughed. Andrew would probably have asked them for a fight.

But we liked eating out. A lot. When we went to a restaurant, the vegetarian option was always mushroom risotto or halloumi kebabs. Andrew – a chef since the age of 16 – would say that he didn't need to see the menu, he knew what was going to be on it already.

So we decided to open our own vegetarian restaurant. We set some standards for the food: no dish would rely on pasta, meat substitutes or heavy spicing. No piles of pulses would be used to bulk up a dish. We would create menus of unusual combinations which challenged the norms. There would be no postcards in the window advertising yoga classes. And we wouldn't follow anyone else's rules. It was a massive adventure to us to leave our jobs and start the restaurant. Andrew had been teaching catering and Donna was nursing.

What we do is different. Someone once said to us that 'you put your head above the parapet and you don't care'. In fact, we would make more money if we served veggie burgers and chips. But we *do* care. We care about making a difference and about breaking the mould.

We opened Vanilla Black in York in December 2004 with one member of staff: a student from the local university. And we started to divide people. We served a savoury Bakewell tart containing chilli jam and a savoury almond sponge, with vegetable vinaigrette. Once, when I took it to a customer, he took one look, got up and walked out. However, slowly we started to attract people (most of them meat-eaters) looking for something interesting.

Almost everyone was very complimentary. But one of the most interesting reactions was from Andrew's father, who apologetically told us that it was a shame that he couldn't come in, 'because I'm not vegetarian'. Finally, after a long session pointing out that cornflakes, tomato soup and cheese on toast were vegetarian, the penny dropped and he came along for a meal. And thoroughly enjoyed it.

But, then, like anything does, running a restaurant became a job… We became restless and we felt we had outgrown our little restaurant. We needed another challenge.

So we decided to move to London. That was certainly a challenge. We knew absolutely nobody there and had only ever visited once or twice as tourists and yet, a few weeks later, we went and had a look around… We liked what we saw and decided to make the move. We were naïve but we weren't arrogant. We weren't under any illusion that we would arrive and all would be rosy and good. But we didn't think it would be as hard as it was.

As we write, we are about to celebrate our tenth anniversary, of which we are very proud. It has been a challenge for us trying to break away from the stereotypes that surround vegetarian cooking. We are not trying to be clever, but the day when our menu is familiar, or comparable to some other style of cooking, and that people don't ask us dozens of questions before ordering their food, is the day we have stagnated. So, before you read this book, you should know this…

'Apologies in advance, no pasta bake or vegetable curry.'

A Footnote

Don't make the mistake that, by buying this book, you are buying a compendium of healthy recipes. A vegetarian diet isn't necessarily any better or worse for your body than any other. You could eat cheese and chips all day long and never let a green vegetable darken your door from one year to the next and still – truthfully – declare yourself to be vegetarian.

A Quick Word About Ingredients

BUTTER

We always use unsalted; that way it doesn't interfere with the flavour balance in sweet dishes. Also, you can then salt any recipe, safe in the knowledge that there is not already some seasoning present. You can always add salt, but you can't take it away.

CHOCOLATE

Try to use good stuff; this is definitely a case of getting what you pay for. Look for a label that says '70% cocoa solids' on dark chocolate, as this will give a good strong flavour, but remember that this only indicates the strength of chocolate, not its quality.

EGGS

For the recipes in this book, use medium free-range eggs. By all means trade up to organic, if you wish.

OVEN

These recipes assume your oven is electric, either conventional or fan-assisted and definitely preheated. They will also work using a gas oven, but you need to be aware that they haven't been tested in one of those, so you will need to take more care, especially with baking recipes, that baking is happening evenly and at a smooth, slowish pace. If you have an Aga, well, lucky you. If you can, try to organise things so that you utilise your oven fully: cook two recipes that require baking at the same time, to save fuel and bills.

SALT

Some people don't believe in adding salt to a dish, believing that it is unhealthy. Salt is not unhealthy, *too much* salt is unhealthy. When we say season something, we mean add a little salt and pepper; you need to use your own judgement about this as we are all different. You can use regular table salt, which dissolves quickly. We tend to use sea salt flakes, because they are not as harsh as table salt and also – for some dishes – the flakes act almost as a garnish, giving little crumbly hits of salt.

SMOKE OIL

This is amazing. It's a naturally flavoured oil which is very intense – a little certainly does go a long way, so be careful. We buy it from a company called MSK Ingredients and you can order it online at msk-ingredients.com. Be careful, this company sells some amazing products and you will be tempted to add lots to your basket.

SUGAR

You will see that we sometimes use different types of sugar in the cakes as they can create different flavour notes. That's it.

SUNFLOWER OIL

This is used in the cake recipes, as it gives a moister sponge. Why? Because part of butter's make-up is water, which is why it spits and splutters when you heat it in a pan. When you add butter to a recipe, you are actually adding a little more water at the same time. When you use oil it contains no water, so the recipe is more stable. Also, when a cake made with oil cools down, the oil prevents the sponge from toughening up. By the way, when any of the recipes in this book ask for 'sunflower oil' you can substitute vegetable oil, if you wish.

...AND A FINAL THING

Don't be a slave to a recipe. If you cannot get hold of a certain sugar, use white granulated. If you are having difficulty finding heritage potatoes, use something else. If the recipe says sultanas and you only have raisins, use them. If you don't have any icing sugar to dust a cake, so what? If a dish calls for cauliflower, make it next time with broccoli, or vice versa. Try swapping cheeses in a recipe, or even mix a couple and see what happens... sometimes the best creations can come from a little experimentation.

Oh, and have fun.

Andrew Dargue and Donna Conroy,
London, 2015

BREAKFAST

Best porridge

The secret to really great porridge is in the oats: toasting them in a little butter before incorporating the milk brings richness and a delicious nutty flavour.

Try it with home-made jam dolloped in the middle of the bowl and sprinkled with some more toasted oats. However, it's just as good with Poached autumn fruits, Sweet pesto (see pages 21 and 115), or just a drizzle of honey.

SERVES 4

20g unsalted butter
150g rolled oats
1 litre whole milk
75g light muscovado sugar
pinch of sea salt
4 tbsp jam (preferably home-made, see page 114)

Melt the butter over a medium heat in the biggest saucepan you have, then add the oats and stir until they're toasted and golden brown. You will smell the toastiness and see the slight colour change; it will only take about 4 minutes. Remove 2 tbsp of oats and set aside on a plate.

Add the milk, sugar and salt to the remaining oats in the saucepan, stirring often so the mixture doesn't catch, for 10–15 minutes, until the oats have swollen to form a thick porridge.

Serve in bowls, sprinkled with the reserved oats and with some of your favourite jam.

Herbed soda bread

This is the perfect recipe for those intimidated by the thought of making bread, because it uses a mix of bicarbonate of soda and baking powder instead of yeast. This means it's faster to make, as you don't need to wait for the yeast to activate; these sorts of loaves were made much more in the past because of this. You can use any herbs you like, but the more robust varieties such as sage, thyme and rosemary flavour the dough best.

The bread is great toasted and served with poached eggs, baked beans and wilted baby spinach.

MAKES 1 SMALL LOAF

3 tbsp olive oil, plus more for the tin
500g strong white bread flour
1½ tsp sea salt, plus 1 tbsp for the top
3 tsp bicarbonate of soda
2 tsp baking powder
1 tbsp granulated sugar
2 tbsp finely chopped mixture of sage and thyme leaves

450ml whole milk

Preheat the oven to 200°C/fan 180°C/gas mark 6. Oil a 26 x 12cm loaf tin and line the base and sides with baking parchment.

Sift the flour, 1½ tsp of salt, the bicarbonate of soda and baking powder into a large mixing bowl and stir in the sugar and herbs.

Make a well in the middle and pour in the milk and 3 tbsp of oil, mixing with your hands for about 5 minutes to gradually incorporate the dry ingredients (or combine in a food mixer fitted with the dough hook attachment). The mix will be very sticky and wet, but keep the faith…

Spoon into the prepared tin – it will need a little bit of encouragement to flatten down a bit – and sprinkle the 1 tbsp of sea salt on top. Bake for 45–50 minutes, or until the loaf is golden brown with a hard crust. Turn out of the tin and cool on a wire rack.

Slice and serve toasted or not, with plenty of good butter.

Breakfast bar

This recipe is gluten- and dairy-free and has a texture similar to that of fruit cake. It's so simple to make and can be prepared in advance for the week. There do seem to be a lot of ingredients, but if you do a lot of baking you will have these things in your cupboards already and, if not, you can improvise as long as the weights are equal to those ingredients you substitute. If you don't have buckwheat flour and you're not aiming for a gluten-free result, use plain flour instead. We have called this a breakfast bar but – if you want to live on the edge a little – eat it at another time of day.

MAKES 8

unsalted butter or sunflower oil, for the tin

50g rolled oats
15g desiccated coconut
40g hazelnuts, chopped
40g walnuts, chopped
40g peanuts, chopped
150g pitted dates, chopped
1 tsp bicarbonate of soda
50g buckwheat flour
25g dried cranberries
25g raisins
50g dried apricots, chopped
50g candied mixed peel
1 ripe banana, mashed
2 tbsp honey
½ tsp ground cinnamon
½ tsp ground ginger
1 tsp baking powder
pinch of sea salt

Preheat the oven to 165°C/fan 145°C/gas mark 3. Butter or oil a 26 x 12cm loaf tin, then line the base and sides with baking parchment.

Spread the oats and desiccated coconut over one non-stick baking tray, and all the chopped nuts over another, then toast in the oven for 10–20 minutes or until golden brown, turning with a spatula every 5 minutes to ensure they cook evenly and don't catch and burn.

Pour 150ml of water into a saucepan, add the dates and bicarb and set over a medium heat until the water has mostly evaporated and the dates have softened, about 5 minutes. The bicarb will turn the dates a dark green colour, but don't be alarmed! Blend them to a smooth purée using a hand-held blender, then combine in a large mixing bowl with all the other ingredients, including the toasted oats, coconut and nuts.

Spoon into the prepared tin and bake for 30–40 minutes or until firm to the touch. Allow to set in the tin for 10 minutes before turning out and leaving to cool completely on a wire rack.

Once cool, cut into 8 thick slices. These will keep very well in an airtight container for up to 1 week.

Muesli crumble

This is not your regular muesli – we have incorporated a crumble into the mix which makes it a bit richer. If you do not have all of the nuts or fruits which are called for in the recipe, don't worry, just substitute them with whatever you do have in the cupboard.

Serve with yogurt and Poached autumn fruits (see page 21), or be adventurous and serve it as a dessert with cream and dark chocolate; go on, it really works. See page 208 for an example of using muesli with dessert.

MAKES 12–15 SERVINGS

300g plain flour
pinch of salt
150g demerara sugar
200g cold unsalted butter, chopped
200g rolled oats
50g desiccated coconut
60g hazelnuts, chopped
60g peanuts, chopped
60g flaked almonds
20g pumpkin seeds
100g dried apricots, chopped
100g pitted dates, chopped
100g pitted prunes, chopped
100g raisins

Preheat the oven to 165°C/fan 145°C/gas mark 3.

Sift the flour and salt into a large mixing bowl and stir in the sugar. Rub in the butter with your fingertips to form a texture like crumbs (or pulse-blend in a food processor to produce the same effect). Mix in the oats and coconut, then spread evenly over a non-stick baking tray.

Bake in the oven for 20–25 minutes or until golden brown, turning with a spatula every 10 minutes to ensure it cooks evenly.

Spread the nuts and pumpkin seeds on a separate non-stick baking tray and toast in the oven at the same time for 15–20 minutes, turning regularly, or until golden.

Allow everything to cool, then mix it all together with the dried fruits. Store in an airtight container for up to 1 month.

VARIATION

For a real energy boost, try substituting the fruits and nuts called for in the main recipe with 75g chopped 70% cocoa solids chocolate, 50g dried cranberries, 50g candied mixed peel, 75g chopped toasted hazelnuts and a sprinkling of cocoa nibs (see page 213).

Poached autumn fruits

Autumn brings an abundance of fruits, the flavours of which are greatly enhanced by gentle poaching. Damsons and quinces work well in this recipe too, if you can get hold of them. It's important to poach each type of fruit separately, as they all cook at slightly different rates.

These are great served at breakfast time, but also make a lovely easy dessert when spooned over vanilla ice cream with a dash of Cointreau.

You can substitute the red wine with cranberry juice if you prefer, though the wine gives richness and depth to the fruit. We have given times for poaching but, as with all food, it's a natural product, so keep your eye on it as times can vary.

If you want to elevate this mixture when you have people to dinner, take a slice of brioche, dust with icing sugar, grill and place on a plate. Spoon some warmed fruits on top, drizzle a little of their syrup around, then top with a spoonful of clotted cream.

SERVES 4

75g golden caster sugar
300ml red wine
7.5cm strip of orange zest, removed with a vegetable peeler

1 clove
2 medium Bramley apples, peeled, cored and each cut into 8 segments

2 Conference pears, peeled, cored and each cut into 8 segments

2 red plums, quartered and pitted
75g blackberries, halved if large

Pour 300ml of water into a large, wide pan and add the sugar, wine, orange zest and clove. Bring to the boil, then reduce the heat to a gentle simmer, add the apple segments and cover, poaching gently for 7–10 minutes until soft and plump. (Don't increase the heat as this will cause the fruit to overcook.) Remove carefully with a slotted spoon to a large bowl. Repeat this process with the pears and plums, cooking each fruit separately and lifting them out when *just* tender. This could take anywhere from a few minutes for ripe plums, to 25 minutes for harder pears, so keep your eye on them.

Discard the orange peel (reserve for decoration if you like) and clove, then increase the heat to reduce the poaching liquid by half.

Place the blackberries in the bowl with the rest of the fruit, then pour over the poaching liquor and allow to sit for 10 minutes before serving.

Smoky baked beans with poached eggs and chive oil

Making your own baked beans is surprisingly gratifying. You can use haricot beans as we do here, or a mix of kidney, butter or black beans depending on what you like the best. They're great for breakfast served with toast or Herbed soda bread (see page 17), but also make a lovely midweek supper. We use smoke oil (see page 11), which makes a fantastic addition to your storecupboard and can be used in a variety of dishes. However, if you don't have any, you can use 1 tsp smoked paprika instead.

_____

SERVES 4

For the chive oil
   10g chives, roughly chopped, plus more
   to serve

   pinch of sea salt
   200ml sunflower oil

For the smoky beans
   3 tbsp sunflower oil
   1 medium onion, finely chopped
   1kg (about 8) tomatoes, roughly chopped
   1 tbsp sea salt
   2 tsp granulated sugar
   pinch of cayenne pepper
   1 tbsp tomato purée
   200ml white wine
   1 bay leaf
   400g can of haricot beans, drained
   and rinsed

   3 tsp smoke oil (see page 11)

For the poached eggs
   4 tbsp salt
   100ml white wine vinegar
   8 eggs

To serve
   4 slices of toast, buttered
   1 tsp sea salt
   150g watercress

Prepare the chive oil by blitzing the chives and salt in the oil using a hand-held blender. You can prepare this the night before, so the chive flavour has time to infuse the oil.

To make the smoky beans, heat the 3 tbsp of oil in a large, heavy-based frying pan or casserole dish and gently sauté the onion over a medium-low heat. Once the onion has softened, add the tomatoes, salt, sugar, cayenne, tomato purée, wine and bay leaf, then stir in 100ml of water and cover. Increase the heat to medium and bring to a simmer. Cook for 15 minutes or until the tomatoes are soft, then remove from the heat.

Discard the bay leaf and blend using a hand-held blender, then pass through a sieve to remove any seeds. Pour into a clean pan and cook over a low heat for about 20 minutes until the sauce has reduced and thickened.

Add the beans to the tomato sauce, along with the smoke oil. Taste and adjust the seasoning if necessary. Keep warm over a low heat until you're ready to serve.

Meanwhile, to prepare the poached eggs, bring a generous amount of water, with the salt and vinegar, to the boil in the largest saucepan you have. Once the water has reached the boil, reduce the heat to low.

Two eggs at a time, crack each into a separate shallow dish or bowl. Using a large slotted spoon, stir the water in a circle, then carefully drop one egg into the centre, then another. The whites should wrap around the yolk while in the vortex, to create a teardrop shape. Allow the eggs to cook for 3–5 minutes, gently stirring the water from time to time to prevent them from settling on the bottom. Once the whites have set, remove to a bowl of cold water with a slotted spoon and repeat the process to cook all the eggs.

When you are ready to serve, return all the poached eggs to the boiling water in the pan to warm through. About 1 minute should do it. Divide the beans over the 4 hot toasts on plates and sit 2 well-drained eggs on each, with a small pinch of sea salt sprinkled on the eggs. Now place a large handful of watercress on top, finishing with a drizzle of chive oil and sprinkling with a few more chopped chives.

Baked duck eggs with tomato and rosemary cake and charred sweetcorn

This makes for a hearty breakfast or brunch at the weekend when you've more time (or guests to impress). If you haven't any white truffle oil you can use Fried onion vinaigrette or Microwave brown sauce (see pages 108 and 102) instead. The tomato and rosemary cake can be prepared the night before, stored in an airtight container and warmed through in a low oven when you're ready to serve. If you happen to have any of the tomato cakes left, keep them for supper, cut them open, add a little grated Cheddar, then grill them.

———————

SERVES 4

For the cakes
    80g/100ml sunflower oil, plus more
    for the moulds and to char the sweetcorn

    2 eggs, lightly beaten
    1 tbsp tomato purée
    80g self-raising flour, sifted
    1 tsp finely chopped rosemary leaves
    ½ tsp sea salt

For the baked eggs
    2 tsp unsalted butter, for the ramekins
    4 duck eggs
    4 tbsp single cream
    freshly ground white pepper

To serve
    150g frozen sweetcorn
    200g baby spinach
    2 tbsp white truffle oil (optional)

Preheat the oven to 155°C/fan 135°C/gas mark 2. Oil four muffin moulds.

To make the tomato and rosemary cakes, whisk the eggs, oil and tomato purée in a large mixing bowl (or mix in a food mixer with the beater attachment), then add the flour, rosemary and salt, mixing until thoroughly combined.

Divide between the muffin moulds and bake for 20–25 minutes or until firm to the touch and a skewer inserted into the middle of a cake comes out clean. Leave in the moulds for 10 minutes, then carefully unmould and leave to cool on a wire rack.

Meanwhile, prepare the baked eggs. Increase the oven temperature to 170°C/fan 150°F/gas mark 3½ and butter 4 ramekins.

Crack an egg into each prepared ramekin. Season the cream with salt and white pepper, then add 1 tbsp to each ramekin, avoiding the egg yolk. Place on a baking tray and bake for 15–20 minutes, removing once the whites have set and the yolk is done to your liking. You may need to spin the baking tray around halfway through to ensure the eggs cook evenly.

While the eggs are cooking, char the sweetcorn. Pour a little oil into a frying pan set over a high heat, then add the frozen sweetcorn and a pinch of salt. Toss it in the hot oil and allow it to burn slightly… be careful as the sweetcorn will pop.

To serve, place a ramekin of baked egg on each plate with a cake and a handful of baby spinach. Scatter the charred sweetcorn around the plate and finish with a drizzle of white truffle oil over the spinach.

TEA AND BISCUITS

Chelsea buns

A little twist on a good old British favourite, as these are made with almonds and mixed peel. Although one of the more time-consuming recipes in this book, these are fun to make at the weekend and well worth the extra effort. The aroma as they bake is incomparable! They are also a good test of your baking skills.

Chelsea buns keep well in the freezer for up to 1 month; you can simply defrost them in the microwave on a low setting for 2 or 3 minutes. If you like, you are welcome to change the dried fruits or the nuts to put your own spin on the recipe.

MAKES 12

For the dough
100ml whole milk
10.5g (3 tsp or 1½ packets) fast-action dried yeast

2 tbsp granulated sugar
500g strong white bread flour, sifted, plus more to dust

15g sea salt
35g unsalted butter, softened
2 eggs, lightly beaten
sunflower oil, for the moulds (optional)

For the filling
150g candied mixed peel
150g flaked almonds
100g light muscovado sugar
100g unsalted butter

For the glaze
25g granulated sugar
1 tbsp vanilla extract

For the dough, warm the milk in a microwave or saucepan with 120ml of water until tepid, then remove from the heat and add the yeast and sugar. Mix thoroughly. Leave covered in a warm place for 10 minutes until frothy.

Using your hands, rub together the flour, salt and chopped butter in a large mixing bowl until the mixture resembles crumbs, then make a well in the middle and pour in the yeast mixture and the eggs, stirring to form a dough. Knead the mixture with your hands, or in a food mixer fitted with the dough hook, for 10 minutes. Put in a bowl, cover with cling film and leave in a warm, draught-free place to prove (rise) for 40 minutes.

Meanwhile, make the filling. Combine the mixed peel, flaked almonds and muscovado sugar in a bowl; melt the butter and set aside.

For the glaze, mix 2 tbsp of boiling water into the sugar and vanilla extract to make a paste.

After the dough has proved, remove it to a large floured worktop and lightly knead for a minute, then split it in half. Don't overwork the dough as this makes it harder to roll out. Using a floured rolling pin (and ensuring your worktop is still well floured), roll out one half of dough into a rectangle, about 45 x 30cm.

Brush some of the melted butter generously over the surface, then cover with half the almond mix, leaving a 1cm border around the edge so the filling doesn't fall out. Now do the same with the other half of the dough.

Starting with the longest edge closest to you, gently roll both pieces of the dough up, brushing with more melted butter on the rolls as you go. When it is all rolled up, ensure the seams are underneath. They should look like big sausage rolls.

Trim the ends with a knife and divide each into six equal-sized buns, then transfer to muffin moulds spiral-side up, gently pressing them down to fit the shape (if your moulds are not made from silicone you will need to oil them lightly). Brush each bun with some of the glaze (reserve the rest). Cover loosely with cling film and return to a warm place for 30–45 minutes, until the buns have grown by one-third.

Preheat the oven to 170°C/fan 150°C/gas mark 3½. Bake for 25–30 minutes, or until the buns are golden brown.

Brush with more vanilla glaze and allow to cool in the moulds for 10 minutes before turning out. Leave on a wire rack, baked sides up, to cool completely.

Butter buns

Essentially a brioche recipe, these light, melt-in-the-mouth buns are great to make at the weekend when you have a bit more time than usual. It is a tricky and time-consuming recipe but, when you see the results, you'll feel like a professional. The dough can be started the night before and left in the fridge to be baked in the morning. Eat them with anything you want: jam, fruit, butter… or how about chocolate spread?

MAKES 12

60ml whole milk
10.5g (3 tsp or 1½ packets) fast-action
dried yeast

45g caster sugar, plus 1 tsp, plus more
to glaze

440g strong white flour, plus more to dust
11g (2 tsp) sea salt
300g/280ml (about 6 medium) eggs,
lightly beaten, plus 1 more to glaze

250g unsalted butter, softened

Warm the milk in a microwave or saucepan until tepid, then add the yeast and 1 tsp of the sugar, mixing thoroughly. Cover and leave in a warm place for 10 minutes until frothy.

Combine the flour, 45g of sugar and salt in a food mixer fitted with a dough hook, or use your hands. Make a well in the middle, add the yeast mixture and eggs and knead for 7 minutes. Now slowly add the butter, 1 heaped tbsp at a time, allowing plenty of kneading after each addition to ensure it is thoroughly incorporated. Regularly scrape the butter from the sides of the bowl back into the dough. Cover with cling film and leave to prove in a warm, draught-free place for 45 minutes.

Knead, just to knock back the dough, for 3 minutes. Put into a bowl, cover with cling film and prove a second time for 30 minutes. (Or, the night before, refrigerate, tightly covered with cling film so it doesn't dry out. In the morning, return to room temperature before working the dough.) Knock the dough back again, then divide into 12 and place each piece in a floured muffin mould (we use silicone but, if you haven't got those,

line the moulds with baking parchment or paper cases first). Cover loosely with cling film and prove for a final time until increased in size by one-third; it should take about 20 minutes.

Preheat the oven to 175°C/fan 155°C/ gas mark 4.

Bake for 10 minutes, then brush the tops with a little beaten egg and a sprinkling of sugar and bake for 3–5 minutes, or until golden brown.

Allow to cool for 10 minutes before serving.

VARIATION

For Easter you can make hot-cross butter buns: add 1 tsp (3g) ground cinnamon to the flour mix and 400g mixed dried fruit after the first proving. To make the cross, form a thick paste from sifted plain flour and water, piping it over the buns before they go in the oven.

Crisp salted toffee biscuits

This recipe has a neat little trick involving chocolate flavoured popped rice cereal; the kernels give an interesting crunch to the biscuits. Be careful when heating the chocolate, as it can burn easily.

MAKES 8

For the biscuits
220g self-raising flour
1 tbsp bicarbonate of soda
80g caster sugar
100g 70% cocoa solids chocolate, finely chopped

2 tbsp cocoa powder
pinch of sea salt
150g unsalted butter, softened
100g golden syrup

For the filling
75g 70% cocoa solids chocolate, chopped

30g chocolate flavour popped rice cereal
1 quantity Salted butterscotch (see page 117; you won't need it all but it keeps well in the fridge)

Preheat the oven to 140°C/fan 120°C/ gas mark 1.

For the biscuits, combine the flour, bicarbonate of soda, sugar, chocolate, cocoa powder and salt in a large mixing bowl (or mix in a food mixer fitted with the beater attachment), then mix in the butter and golden syrup, beating until thoroughly combined.

Divide into 16 balls (about 1 heaped tbsp each), placing them evenly over 2 baking trays lined with baking parchment, then bake for 25–30 minutes. You may need to turn the tray around halfway through to ensure the biscuits cook evenly in the oven.

Place the baking tray on a cooling rack and leave to cool.

Meanwhile, make the filling. Melt the chocolate in a microwave on a low setting, stirring often, or place in a heatproof bowl and melt over a pan of simmering water (the bowl should not touch the water). Add the cereal and mix so the pieces are completely coated in chocolate.

Once the biscuits are cool, carefully remove them with a palette knife. Turn two of them upside-down and spread 1 tbsp of the chocolate filling on one biscuit and 1 tbsp of Salted butterscotch on another, then sandwich the 2 together. Repeat to sandwich all the biscuits.

Leave the biscuits for 30 minutes, to set the filling, before eating.

Shortbread cake

This is essentially a shortbread but, when you add self-raising flour instead of plain flour, the texture changes and becomes lighter and more crumbly. The French call it *sablé Breton* so, if you hear somebody talking about that, you can give a knowing look. Serve it with your choice of fruits and cream. To take it up a notch, bake in individual moulds, split the cakes in half, fill with cream and fruit, then place on a serving plate and top with more fruit... but let it tumble on to the plate so it looks natural.

SERVES 10–12

320g unsalted butter, softened, plus more for the tin

320g golden caster sugar
8 egg yolks
450g self-raising flour
pinch of sea salt
icing sugar, to dust

Preheat the oven to 155°C/fan 135°C/ gas mark 2. Butter a 23cm springform cake tin and line the base with baking parchment.

Cream the butter and sugar together in a large mixing bowl until light and creamy (or use an electric whisk or a food mixer fitted with the beater attachment), then gradually incorporate the egg yolks. Add the flour and salt, mixing until thoroughly combined.

Press evenly into the prepared tin with the back of a spoon and bake for 55–60 minutes or until golden brown.

Leave to cool for 10 minutes, then carefully release the catch and turn out on to a wire rack. It will sink in the middle, but this is normal and, if you are serving it as a dessert, you can put whipped cream, berries and liqueur in the hollow.

Otherwise, when you're ready to serve, just finish with a dusting of icing sugar.

VARIATION

For a chocolate chip shortbread cake, add 150g chopped 70% cocoa solids chocolate with the dry ingredients.

Gypsy creams

Our version of the nostalgic British biscuit, these make a legendary addition to any tea break. You can also try them filled with White chocolate icing or Salted butterscotch (see pages 142 and 117). Or, if you can't be bothered to make either of those, just have the biscuits as they are and dip them in your tea.

MAKES 10

For the biscuits
75g rolled oats
2 tbsp desiccated coconut
220g self-raising flour
1 tbsp bicarbonate of soda
80g granulated sugar
2 tbsp cocoa powder
pinch of sea salt
150g unsalted butter, softened
100g golden syrup

For the filling
100g unsalted butter, softened
50g full-fat cream cheese
100g icing sugar, sifted
50g cocoa powder, sifted

Preheat the oven to 165°C/fan 145°C/gas mark 3.

Spread the oats and coconut on a baking tray and bake for 15–20 minutes, or until golden brown, turning once or twice with a spatula so they cook evenly. Set aside to cool.

Reduce the oven temperature to 140°C/ fan 120°C/gas mark 1.

To make the biscuits, mix the flour, bicarbonate of soda, sugar, oats, coconut, cocoa powder and salt in a large mixing bowl (or use a food mixer fitted with the beater attachment), then beat in the butter and golden syrup.

Divide into 20 balls (about 1 heaped tbsp each), placing them evenly over two baking trays lined with baking parchment, then bake for 25–30 minutes. You may need to turn the tray around halfway through to ensure they cook evenly in the oven. Place the tray on a cooling rack and leave to cool.

For the filling, ensure the butter and cream cheese are at room temperature, which will reduce the risk of any lumps forming. Beat together the butter and cream cheese in a large mixing bowl (or use a food mixer fitted with the beater attachment), then add the icing sugar and cocoa, beating until thoroughly combined.

Once the biscuits are cool, carefully remove them with a palette knife. Turn half of them over and spread a thick layer of buttercream on the flat sides, then sandwich together with the flat sides of the remaining biscuits.

Very jammy biscuits

The original name for the version of these biscuits that is sold commercially comes from a *Beano* comic book character called Roger the Dodger, who I believe was quite jammy. If you are feeling adventurous or reckless you could change the jam for another flavour. Apricot, maybe. Roger won't mind.

―――――――――

MAKES 8

For the biscuits
　　200g cold unsalted butter, chopped
　　200g plain flour
　　100g caster sugar, plus more
　　to sprinkle

　　pinch of sea salt

For the filling
　　75g unsalted butter, softened
　　½ vanilla pod, split, seeds scraped out
　　75g icing sugar, sifted
　　8 tsp raspberry jam (preferably
　　home-made)

Preheat the oven to 140°C/fan 120°C/gas mark 1. The low temperature is intentional, so the shortbread sets slowly and cooks evenly.

Rub the butter into the flour, sugar and salt in a large mixing bowl until you have a texture like crumbs. Or you can pulse the ingredients together in a food processor instead. Now form it into a dough with your hands (you might need a splash of water to help it come together).

Divide the mix in 2 and lightly shape each into a log about 6cm in diameter (don't overwork the mixture). Wrap in cling film and chill in the fridge for 1 hour. Once firm, cut each into 8 circles and space them evenly over 2 large baking trays lined with baking parchment, a small distance away from each other as they will spread slightly.

Bake for 35–40 minutes or until a light golden brown. You may need to turn the trays around halfway through to ensure the biscuits cook evenly in the oven.

As soon as the biscuits come out of the oven, cut a hole in the centre of half of them with a 3cm cutter, or the smallest cutter you have. (You can also cut them out once more with a 6cm cutter if you want to tidy up the edges.) Place the baking tray on a cooling rack and leave to cool.

Meanwhile, make the filling. Beat the butter and vanilla seeds in a large mixing bowl (or in a food mixer fitted with the beater attachment), then beat in the icing sugar until thoroughly combined.

Once the biscuits are cool, carefully remove them with a palette knife. Turn the intact biscuits upside-down and gently spread the buttercream over, leaving a space in the middle of each for 1 tsp of jam. Add the jam. Sandwich together with the biscuits with the holes and sprinkle with caster sugar.

Rum and raisin biscuits

Often a 'rum and raisin' recipe will ask for rum essence but it's nowhere near as good as the real thing that we use here and, because of that, these biscuits have a bit more of a kick. There is a warning in the recipe which says not to overwork the buttercream, so take heed because – if you walk away and leave it to its own devices – you will come back to a scrambled mess.

MAKES 8

For the biscuits
220g self-raising flour
1 tbsp bicarbonate of soda
80g light muscovado sugar
50g raisins
pinch of sea salt
150g unsalted butter, softened
100g golden syrup

For the filling
100g unsalted butter, softened
50ml dark rum
100g icing sugar, sifted

Preheat the oven to 140°C/fan 120°C/gas mark 1.

For the biscuits, combine the flour, bicarbonate of soda, sugar, raisins and salt in a large mixing bowl (or use a food mixer fitted with the beater attachment), then mix in the butter and golden syrup until thoroughly combined.

Divide into 16 balls (about 1 heaped tbsp each), placing them evenly over 2 baking trays lined with baking parchment, then bake for 25–30 minutes or until golden brown. You may need to turn the tray around halfway through to ensure they cook evenly in the oven. Place the baking tray on a cooling rack and leave to cool.

To make the buttercream, beat the butter in a large mixing bowl (or use a food mixer fitted with the beater attachment), then gradually add the rum. Now add the icing sugar and beat again until thoroughly combined. Be careful not to overwork the buttercream, as it will likely split.

Once the biscuits are cool, carefully remove them with a palette knife. Turn half of them over and spread a thick layer of buttercream on the flat sides, then sandwich together with the flat sides of the remaining biscuits.

Jacket potato soup with chive sour cream

This is so hearty that you could turn it into a meal by serving it with Leek and Cheddar Welsh rarebit (see page 149). To save your energy bills, it's best to cook the potatoes when you are using the oven for something else; you can always keep the cooked potatoes in the fridge for two days until you are ready to make the soup. Whipping cream makes the soup a little bit lighter than double cream would. You can elevate the recipe by adding a poached egg to the bowl, ladling the soup over the top and then adding the chive sour cream. Keeping the egg soft-poached, so it pops when you cut into it, makes a nice surprise at the bottom of the bowl.

SERVES 4

1kg baking potatoes (you won't be able to get this weight exactly due to the random size of the potatoes, but close to 1kg will do; it's about 4)

50g unsalted butter
1 large onion, finely chopped
2 tbsp chopped chives
100g sour cream
sea salt and freshly ground black pepper

125ml whipping cream, plus more if needed (optional)

whole milk, if needed (optional)

Preheat the oven to 230°C/fan 210°C/gas mark 8. Scrub the potatoes and bake for 1 hour, or until tender when pierced with a knife. When they are cool, carefully peel with a small knife, not a peeler. Keep the skins. Chop the potato flesh roughly; don't be fussy, you are going to blend it later.

Pour 750ml of water into a pan, add the skins and simmer for 10 minutes. Allow to cool in the pan.

Melt the butter in a separate large saucepan and gently cook the onion until nice and soft, but not coloured. Strain the water from the potato skins through a sieve and add it to the pan with the onion. You can throw the skins away now, there's not much more you can do with them. Now add the potato flesh and gently simmer for 10 minutes.

Meanwhile add the chives to the sour cream, season and mix.

Remove the soup from the heat and blend with a hand-held blender, being careful of hot splashes. When it is nice and smooth, reheat if needed, then add the whipping cream. Do not simmer or boil once the cream is added, as it could split. Depending on the starch content of your potatoes, you may need to adjust the consistency of the soup with milk.

Serve, adding a dollop of the chive sour cream at the last minute so it sits on top of the soup.

Celeriac, golden raisin, celery and horseradish yogurt salad

A real punchy salad with plenty of earthy flavours, just balanced by the sweet raisins. Do try to find fresh horseradish if you can; just the experience of grating it is something you will remember for some time… be prepared for tears. Despite its name it has not a lot to do with horses – the word 'horse' was once used as a term for something that was coarse or strong. A spoonful of this salad would be great dropped into Jacket potato soup (see page 48), or as a side dish with Baked beetroot with home-made curds and toasted sunflower seeds (see page 148).

SERVES 6

25g fresh horseradish (or
2 tbsp horseradish sauce)

200ml good-quality natural yogurt
1 small celeriac
2 celery stalks, very finely chopped
80g golden raisins
sea salt and freshly ground
black pepper

Peel the horseradish with a small knife, then grate it finely. Wash your hands afterwards. The grated root will seem very strong, but don't worry, it does calm down. Mix the horseradish with the yogurt.

Peel the celeriac (for the easiest way, see the recipe introduction opposite) and grate it coarsely so you have some texture. Place in a bowl. Add the celery and raisins, then the horseradish yogurt. Season and mix; the result will resemble coleslaw.

The salad does not keep too long as the celeriac tends to discolour, so try to use it the same day.

Next time, try using some sliced green apple in place of celery for an interesting hit of freshness.

Celeriac and apple soup with walnut oil

This is such an easy but impressive soup to make. It requires minimum input, but the end result is an intriguing flavour... so maximum Brownie points. Because the celeriac has a taste of celery, the walnut oil pairs very well, while the apples help to add a little acid and balance the flavours – that's why we use tart Granny Smiths. Make a double batch of walnut oil; it keeps well in the fridge and can be used for salads and other soups. If you have never peeled a celeriac before, cut through the top to make four wedges first; this will make it easier to handle. And use a knife instead of a peeler, as the skin is quite thick.

SERVES 6

50g unsalted butter
1 small onion, finely chopped
1 large celeriac, peeled and chopped
(it may seem a lot but you lose some in
the peeling)

1 potato, peeled and roughly chopped
2 Granny Smith apples, peeled, cored
and roughly chopped

1 celery stalk, finely chopped
750ml vegetable stock or water
(there is a lot of flavour in this soup
so water is OK)

80g walnuts
100ml sunflower oil (you can use olive oil,
but we find it overpowering)

125ml whole milk, plus more if needed
125ml whipping cream
sea salt and freshly ground black pepper

In a large saucepan, melt the butter and cook the onion on a low heat, without colouring it. Next add the celeriac, potato, apples and celery. Pour in the stock or water. Depending on the size of your pan you may find that some of the vegetables are sticking out of the liquid – if so, add water to just cover, but don't go too far as the vegetables will settle down as they cook. Cover and gently simmer for 20–25 minutes until the vegetables are soft.

Meanwhile, make the walnut oil: smash the walnuts a little with the end of a rolling pin just to break them up. Heat a dry frying pan, add the walnuts and dry-fry them quickly, making sure you stir to prevent them burning. This will give a nice roasted flavour to the end result. Turn off the heat and add the oil to the pan – be careful as it may spit – then allow to cool.

Transfer to a clean container until needed (it will keep for 2 weeks in the fridge).

Use a hand-held blender to blend the soup until it is very smooth – it will thicken up because of the starch in the potato.

Now add the milk and cream and reheat, but do not boil as it could split. Depending on how starchy your potato was, your soup may be a bit on the thick side; if so add a little more milk. Season and make sure you use a good few grinds of pepper.

Serve in warmed bowls with a drizzle of walnut oil and some nice nutty wholemeal bread.

We find that some crumbled blue Stilton makes this soup a bit special, especially as it starts to melt into the soup.

Broad bean, spring onion and lemon cheesecake

For this recipe we use fresh beans; you can use frozen but, in the summer, the fresh variety are so easy to get hold of that it's nice to make use of them. For a variation, try substituting the broad beans with peas and some chopped mint leaves. This dish can be varied many times with a bit of imagination: try making individual versions if you have the moulds, they look delightful as a starter with a mixed leaf salad. They will take a shorter time to bake, so keep an eye on them.

SERVES 6

For the base
75g plain flour
25g toasted porridge oats (see page 14)
50g unsalted butter, chopped
sea salt and freshly ground black pepper

For the filling
250g broad beans, shelled weight (about 750g with the pods)

8 spring onions, trimmed and finely sliced

a little sunflower oil
2 eggs
325g cream cheese
2 tbsp whipping cream
finely grated zest of 1 unwaxed lemon
large punnet of pea shoots, or watercress if you cannot find pea shoots

Preheat the oven to 160°C/fan 140°C/gas mark 3.

Rub together the flour, oats and butter until the mixture resembles crumbs, or just pulse-blend in a food processor. Season with the salt and pepper.

Line a 20cm springform tin with greaseproof paper and press the oat mixture into the base, making sure that there are no gaps. This will save any custard escaping later. Line with another sheet of greaseproof paper and fill with baking beans or raw rice. Blind-bake for 12 minutes, until slightly golden. Set aside.

Set a large pan of water to boil with 1 tsp of salt. Have a bowl of cold water ready. When the water boils, add the beans, cook for 2 minutes, then, using a slotted spoon, remove and add to the cold water to stop the cooking. When they are cooled, we peel them... this is a bit fiddly and time-consuming, so you will be OK to use them as they are if you like, unless you have some spare time. Drain and set aside. Preheat the oven to 140°C/fan 120°C/gas mark 1.

Fry the spring onions in a little oil until just soft.

Beat the eggs and mix in the cream cheese, cream and lemon zest. Now carefully fold in the broad beans and spring onions and season well. Spread evenly over the base and bake for 30–40 minutes, or until set. Allow to cool a little so it is easier to cut, or cool completely and serve cold.

To serve, carefully release from the tin, slice and serve with a mound of pea shoots. This works well with a tomato and mint salad on the side.

Charred asparagus and quail's eggs with peas and lime

Asparagus is a curious thing, it comes and goes so quickly. The official season is 23 April until 21 June... but some people are a bit precious about this. Asparagus does not suddenly become tasteless and woody on 22 June so, if it is still around afterwards, why not use it? It also gets cheaper as the season continues. Eggs and asparagus are a classical pairing but, as ever, we like to add a twist. Using quail's eggs makes the dish seem elegant and enticing – you could even eat it as a fancy starter – but of course you could always use hen's or duck's eggs. And you could poach the eggs instead of boiling them, if you fancy that.

If you can get hold of some pea shoots, sprinkle them on top; their taste shouts summer and they look pretty, too. The lime helps to balance the richness of the dish and is a nice change from lemon.

Have an egg timer ready, or set the timer on your phone... times have changed.

SERVES 4

For the dressing
> finely grated zest and juice of 1 lime
> ½ tsp caster sugar, plus more for the peas
> sprinkle of sea salt, plus more for the peas and to serve
>
> 100ml sunflower oil (you can use olive oil, but we find it overpowering), plus more for the asparagus

For the rest
> 2 packs of 12 quail's eggs (you only need 20, but if some break at least you will not run short)
>
> 2 bunches of asparagus
> 250g frozen peas

57

First make the dressing to allow the sugar and salt time to dissolve. In a bowl, mix the lime zest and juice thoroughly with the sugar and salt. Whisk in the oil and set aside.

Set a pan of water on to boil – about 1 litre should do it. Put all the eggs on a couple of large spoons, to make sure you can get them into the pan quickly instead of one by one. Have a bowl of cold water ready.

When the water comes to the boil, carefully add the eggs and boil for exactly 2 minutes 45 seconds. Transfer with a slotted spoon to the bowl of cold water to stop the cooking. If the water becomes warm because of the hot eggs, drain and add more cold water. When the eggs are cold, carefully peel them.

Preheat the oven to 120°C/fan 100°C/ gas mark ½.

Slice off the bottom 2cm of each asparagus spear, as this can be woody. Heat a large dry frying pan or griddle pan. Making sure the

pan is very hot, add the asparagus in a single layer (you may have to do this in batches) and shake it around so it becomes scorched. Be careful, it can catch quickly. When all the spears are charred, put in a shallow baking tray, sprinkle with a little sunflower oil and place in the oven for 5 to 8 minutes.

Meanwhile, place the peas straight from the freezer into a bowl with a sprinkle of salt and sugar to lift their natural sweetness. Boil a kettle of water and use this to cover the peas generously. Frozen peas are already slightly cooked and this method ensures they still have a fresh flavour. Leave the peas in the water until ready to serve.

To serve, drain the peas and divide between four plates, arranging the asparagus on top. Give the dressing a good stir to emulsify, then spoon it over the vegetables. Add 5 quail's eggs to each plate… unless you were quite a successful peeler and there were no casualties, in which case add the rest. Now sprinkle with sea salt to season the eggs and asparagus.

You may want some bread alongside to mop up the good bits.

Pear, chicory, Stilton and walnut salad with warm potatoes

It's always interesting to see what a difference a warm ingredient makes to a salad. It just seems to transform it into a thoroughgoing meal, and it's easy to do. Balance is the secret to this salad, as it is with all food pairings. You have the rich cheese and nuts against the bitterness of the chicory and the sweetness of the pears. The potatoes form an earthy base for the flavours and cause a bit of wilting and melting, as they are warm, almost cooking the salad slightly. Pears are a tricky, annoying fruit: under-ripe and they are hard and tasteless; over-ripe and they turn to mush. We recommend buying them slightly under-ripe and keeping them for a couple of days until they are just right: they should give a little as you squeeze them – that is the sign that they have reached the right sweetness for this dish. If you cannot get hold of chicory, try red radicchio instead.

You can vary this dish by allowing the potatoes to cool and then frying them in sunflower oil until golden, before adding to the salad.

SERVES 6

250g baby potatoes
sea salt
1 quantity walnut oil (see page 52)
2 heads of white chicory
2 Conference pears, or your own choice, but Conference are reliable

squeeze of lemon juice (optional)
300g Stilton, crumbled

Boil the potatoes in a large saucepan of salted water until just tender when pierced with a knife. Remove from the water with a slotted spoon and lay them on a plate to cool. You will find that cooking them this way keeps the flavour. (You can keep the hot water, as you may need to reheat the potatoes.)

Make the walnut oil as on page 52. If it is still warm when it comes to serving don't worry, it will add to the overall effect, just as long as it is not hot.

Cut 1cm from the base of each head of chicory to help separate the leaves. Separate the leaves, rinse under cold water and pat dry on kitchen paper: there's nothing worse than a watery salad.

Quarter and core the pears, then, using a small knife, slice each quarter into three wedges. You can drop them in a bowl of cold water with a squeeze of lemon juice to prevent discoloration but, if you are using them pretty much straight away, they are OK to hang around for a while.

To serve, reheat the potatoes in their cooking water (unless they are still hot, in which case that will have saved you a job).

If you have serving bowls they would be useful but, if not, plates will be fine. Divide half the chicory between six bowls, add the potatoes, then the rest of the chicory, then the pears. Top with the Stilton. Now spoon over the walnut oil, add a sprinkle of sea salt and serve.

Mix the salad as you eat, so the potatoes help to wilt the chicory and melt the cheese.

Leek, lemon and pine nut tart with wilted wild garlic

Leeks are a great vegetable, although they are known as 'poor man's asparagus'. This seems unfair, as they can hold their own against the posh spears any day. Try serving this tart with wild garlic; if you can find the leaves at farmer's markets, take the opportunity to buy more than you need, as they are quite versatile and interesting. Try slicing them thinly and adding to a soup just before serving, or toss in warm oil and fold into pasta. Or fold them into scrambled eggs when they are cooking and serve on hot buttered toast. If you cannot find any wild garlic, substitute with spinach and a finely chopped garlic clove; not the same but still tasty.

You can add little touches depending on the occasion, situation or your general mood. Perhaps balance a fried egg on top, or sprinkle with grated cheese. A nice fresh Kohlrabi, gherkin and apple salad (see page 182) would complete the meal.

SERVES 4

60g unsalted butter
4 large leeks, peeled, trimmed
and washed

finely grated zest and juice
of 1 unwaxed lemon

sea salt and freshly ground black pepper
plain flour, to dust
250g packet of puff pastry
100g pine nuts, toasted
1 tbsp sunflower oil
200g wild garlic, washed
(or 200g baby leaf spinach and
1 garlic clove, finely chopped)

In a large frying pan, melt the butter over a medium heat. While it melts, cut each leek into four lengths so that you finish with 16 lengths, trying to keep them as equal in size as possible. (Keeping them this size as opposed to in small discs prevents them from falling apart.)

When the butter has melted and has stopped bubbling and hissing, add the leeks to the pan with the lemon zest and juice. Season well. Keep the heat on medium to prevent the leeks catching or falling apart. Allow them to gently bubble in the butter and their own juices, which will start to appear, giving them a turn every 3 minutes so they cook evenly; they should be ready in 12–15 minutes.

To tell if the leeks are cooked, pierce them with a knife: they should be soft to the centre. Nothing worse than undercooked leeks. Set aside in the butter and juices.

Preheat the oven to 180°C/fan 160°C/ gas mark 4.

Meanwhile, prepare the pastry. On a lightly floured worktop, roll out the pastry to a 30 x 20cm rectangle or thereabouts – this does allow for a little waste.

Now slice the rectangle into four smaller rectangles; we find using one of those pizza cutters is really good for cutting pastry. Take a baking tray with low sides which is able to fit the four pastry rectangles.

Lay four lengths of leek next to each other on the tray, almost as if you are trying to create a rectangle that is a similar size to the pastry but a little smaller. This sounds strange but trust me.

Next spoon 1 tbsp of the buttery lemon stock on each leek rectangle, don't worry if it runs off. Now sprinkle on most of the pine nuts; keep some to use as a garnish.

Lay a sheet of pastry on top of each pile of leeks. The pastry should be a little larger than the leeks; it if isn't just push the leeks a little closer together.

Bake in the hot oven for 10–12 minutes; the pastry should be golden and risen. Remove from the oven and allow to settle.

Using the same frying pan to save washing up, discard the remaining leek stock and butter, but do not wash or rinse the pan; some of the flavour will help.

Add the sunflower oil to the pan, heat until the spitting subsides, then add the wild garlic and season. It will seem like a lot of greens but will soon wilt down; turn it in the pan with a wooden spoon to ensure it is cooked equally. If you are using spinach, add the chopped garlic first for a minute, stirring, then continue to wilt the spinach in the same way.

To serve, slide a fish slice under a tart to make sure you catch all the leeks and very carefully turn it so that the pastry becomes the base; use your hand to guide it but be careful of the hot butter and juices. (Baking it this upside-down way ensures that you have a crispy base.)

Place each tart on a plate and sprinkle with the remaining pine nuts. Arrange the wilted garlic (or spinach) on top, or serve it alongside.

Heritage tomatoes and Yorkshire Fettle on toast

If you can get hold of heritage tomatoes, they make this simple dish more interesting. Yorkshire Fettle is a cheese which is really an English feta and is less salty than the Greek version. It was initially called Yorkshire feta but there is a story/myth/legend/fib that the European Union had to intervene and inform the cheese company that it could not use the name 'feta' as it was not made in Greece. They came up with the name Yorkshire Fettle, fettle being an old English term referring to something or someone who is in good shape. This recipe uses the Herbed soda bread from page 17, but if you don't have time some thick granary will do.

SERVES 4

50ml olive oil
sea salt and freshly ground black pepper
small bunch of curly parsley
2 shallots, or 1 small red onion
4 large heritage tomatoes (if you cannot find them try to get the best you can)
caster sugar
4 thick slices of Herbed soda bread (see page 17)
250g Yorkshire Fettle, crumbled

First, marinate the shallots. In a shallow bowl, put the olive oil and a sprinkle of sea salt.

Now chop the parsley, not too fine; keep some texture, as it is a main element here and you want to distinguish it at the end. Add it to the oil.

Next peel and slice the shallots or onion very finely, then add to the parsley oil and mix. Leave to marinate while you do the rest.

Slice the tomatoes around 5mm thick. Lay on a plate and sprinkle with sea salt, pepper and a little sugar; this will heighten the sweetness and help to soften the tomatoes a little.

Heat the grill and toast the slices of bread on one side – you will smell the herbs as it gets hot. Turn over, add the cheese and put it back under the grill. The cheese will not melt but will soften; this is part of the charm.

When it has softened, remove from the grill and top with slices of tomato, then the shallots and parsley. Add a spoon of the oil as well, as it will have picked up lots of flavour, then serve.

If you are lucky the sun will be shining and you can enjoy this with a glass of pale ale.

Cauliflower sheep's cheese with fried mustard crumbs

We use a hard sheep's cheese from the Ribblesdale Cheese Company. It's a really small cheese-making operation in Yorkshire and – at last count – they had a full staff of two and a half. Matured sheep's cheese has a complex flavour and tends to be less greasy than cow's milk cheese; some say it is almost pecorino-like. The breadcrumbs bring a welcome crunch to the dish and the mustard helps to cut through the rich sauce. Do make sure you drain the cauliflower well after it has cooled, as it tends to retain liquid in the florets and can make your sauce watery.

This dish would pair well with Little Marmite potatoes (see page 186) or something a little fresh and acidic such as Kohlrabi, gherkin and apple salad (see page 182) to give balance.

SERVES 4

1 cauliflower
sea salt and freshly ground black pepper
100g unsalted butter
100g plain flour
300ml whole milk
200ml whipping cream
a little sunflower oil
60g breadcrumbs (make your own from
stale bread, or just buy some)

½ tsp English mustard powder
½ tsp dried thyme (or fresh, but dried is faster)
300g sheep's cheese, cut into around
1cm cubes, but don't be fussy

Tear the outer leaves from the cauliflower, discard them and keep the light green inner leaves for later. Bring a pan of lightly salted water to the boil.

Meanwhile, stand the cauliflower upright and cut it into eight wedges. Add to the boiling water and cook for 5 or 6 minutes, or until tender but definitely not soft. Have a bowl of cold water ready.

Remove the cauliflower from the water with a slotted spoon (reserve the hot cooking water) and plunge into the bowl of cold water to stop it cooking. If the cold water gets warm because of the cauliflower, simply add more cold. When it has cooled, throw the cold water away and let the cauliflower drain very well in a colander. Move it around occasionally to drain off any water trapped in the flower.

While the cauliflower drains, you can make the sauce. In a saucepan, melt the butter and then add the flour. Cook for a minute or two until the flour is sandy in texture, stirring all the time to prevent sticking.

Next add 300ml of cauliflower water a little at a time, stirring continuously. This will give some extra cauliflower flavour to the sauce.

Now add the milk and cream a little at a time and cook for a minute, but do not boil, then remove from the heat and allow to cool for around 10 minutes. We don't want to stir in the cubed cheese now – it should melt in the oven so that there are little spots of melted cheese running through the sauce, hence the 10-minute wait.

Preheat the oven to 200°C/fan 180°C/ gas mark 6.

While you wait for the sauce to cool, put a drizzle of sunflower oil in a frying pan – just a couple of tbsp should do it – and fry the breadcrumbs for around 5 minutes over a medium heat. Add the mustard and thyme and fry for another minute, then season and remove from the heat.

Next, fold the cheese into the sauce and season it well.

Arrange the cauliflower in an ovenproof ceramic dish, hopefully one which is pretty enough to be presented at the table. Spoon the sauce over so it covers the cauliflower.

Sprinkle the breadcrumbs on top and bake for 10 minutes; you are not cooking this but rather crisping up the breadcrumbs and melting the cheese. Also your sauce will still be warm, so you have a head start.

Quickly fry the light-green inner leaves reserved earlier in a little oil until tender. Season well.

To serve, either present it in the cooking dish or spoon out on to plates, trying to make sure the breadcrumbs do not disappear under the sauce. Add the cooked cauliflower leaves; they are tastier than you might imagine.

Fried duck egg, sweetcorn pancake, pickles and watercress

The sweetcorn goes well with the rich duck egg and, because both the egg and pancake are fried, the sharpness of the pickles and the bite of the watercress help to balance this dish. You can of course use a hen's egg, but we feel duck's eggs provide more of a focal point. Sprinkle sea salt flakes on your eggs at the end; they crumble as you eat.

Try frying a finely chopped red onion and adding it to the pancake batter, for a delicious variation.

SERVES 4

For the pancakes
   2 eggs
   210ml whole milk
   120g self-raising flour
   100g frozen sweetcorn
   sea salt and freshly ground
   black pepper
   sunflower oil

For the rest
   4 duck's eggs
   small jar of mixed pickles
   of your choice, roughly chopped
   4 handfuls of watercress

Whisk together the eggs, milk and flour until smooth, then add the sweetcorn and season well. (Don't bother defrosting the sweetcorn, it will sort itself out.)

Heat a large frying pan with a little sunflower oil. When the oil is hot, pour in the batter, allow to set for about 20 seconds, then reduce the heat to low to prevent burning. You do want to colour the pancake, but using a low heat will ensure it cooks thoroughly.

When the top of the pancake starts to set a little, use a slice to turn it over (carefully so it does not break), increase the heat to medium and cook for 2 minutes. Or you can invert the pan on to a large plate, then slide the pancake back in, for safety. But I prefer the adrenaline rush… Peek underneath to check if it is golden; if so it's done.

Transfer the pancake to a plate, cut into four wedges and pop under a low grill to keep warm.

Next, wipe the frying pan with kitchen paper – this will save washing it up – then add 2 tbsp of sunflower oil ready for the duck eggs.

Heat the oil and crack each egg into a different area of the pan. Keep over a medium heat until the whites are just set, which is the way we cook them (the soft yolk helps to dress the watercress at the end), or flip each egg over to cook a little more… the choice is yours.

Place the pancake wedges on warmed plates, top each with an egg, sprinkle the eggs with a pinch of sea salt, scatter pickles on top, then add a loose handful of watercress.

Red onion, vintage Cheddar and sage pasty

You can't beat a proper cheese and onion pasty and, when served with piquant Microwave brown sauce (see page 102) it balances the pasty's richness and screams 'British'. You can always make more, as these are good cold and you could take one to work.

Next time try different cheeses... better still, if you have a few different cheeses in the fridge, try a cocktail of two or three: a cheese cocktail pasty.

MAKES 4

3 large baking potatoes (or 600g leftover cooked potato or mash)

50g unsalted butter
2 red onions, finely chopped
250g vintage Cheddar, grated
10 sage leaves, finely chopped
sea salt and freshly ground black pepper
500g packet puff pastry (use ready-rolled if you are short of time)

plain flour, to dust
2 egg yolks, beaten with a splash of whole milk

If you are starting with uncooked potatoes, pierce them with a fork and cook them on high power in the microwave for 15–20 minutes, or until tender when pierced with a knife. Turn them every 5 minutes. Cooking them in the microwave instead of boiling them means that they do not soak up any water and therefore keep all of their flavour. Leave until they are cool enough to handle.

While they cool, melt the butter in a large saucepan (it may seem strange to use a large saucepan but it will become your mixing bowl and therefore save washing up) and gently cook the onions until soft but without colour, then remove from the heat.

With a small knife, peel the potatoes; the skin will come off easily.

Add the peeled potatoes to the saucepan (or add your ready-cooked potato now if you are using leftovers) and mash with a potato masher. Don't be too particular, as sometimes a few lumps give character. Remove from the heat.

Now fold in the cheese and sage and season well. Don't be tempted to eat any of this, though it will be calling you; it's for the pasties. Preheat the oven to 170°C/fan 150°C/gas mark 3½.

Roll out the pastry on a floured worktop until large enough to make four x 20cm circles. Cut them out, then divide the filling between the middles of the circles. Brush egg around the edge of one side of each pastry circle, then bring both sides up and crimp together so the crimp runs along the top.

Brush the pasties with the egg, then sprinkle them with sea salt; don't overdo it, you just want a few salt crunchies at the end. Place on a baking sheet and bake for 20–30 minutes, or until golden brown.

Allow to cool a little and serve warm, or cool and eat later. (Even if you're starving, wait, as straight out of the oven they can be volcanically hot.)

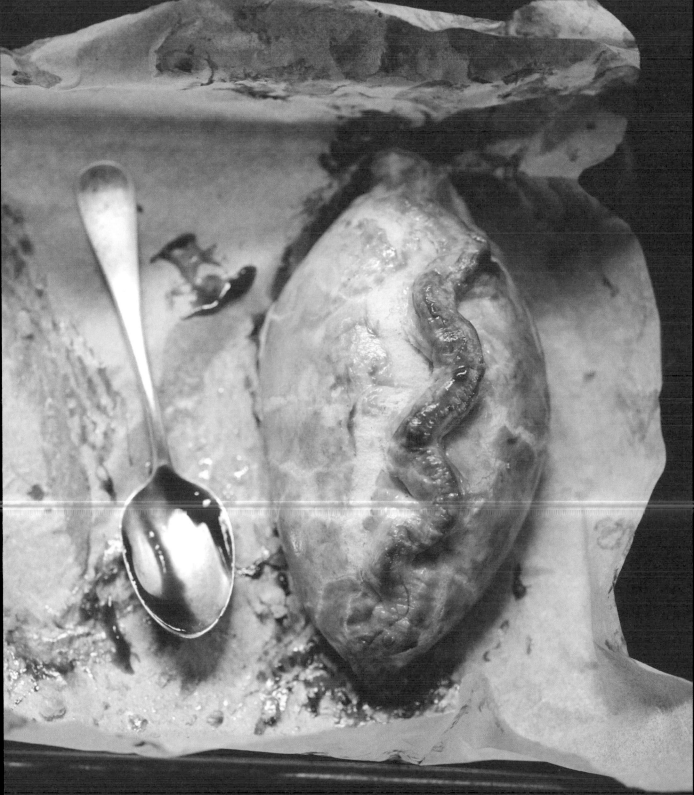

PACKED LUNCHES AND PICNICS

Strawberry, mint and tomato salad

It may seem strange to pair strawberries and tomatoes, but technically they are both fruits. When you can get sweet tomatoes at the height of summer, their slight acidity balances well with the strawberries (tomatoes run the risk of being a bit too acidic at other times of year). For a true summer feel we add mint, which always makes good friends with both tomatoes and strawberries. A chunk of crusty bread and a glass of chilled white wine are probably the only other two ingredients you will need to go with this.

You can tinker with the recipe by changing the vinegar in the dressing. Balsamic, white wine or even cider vinegar will make their personalities felt in different ways. And, next time, add a good few grinds of black pepper or a little chopped chilli, for added warmth.

SERVES 4

25ml good olive oil
2 tbsp raspberry vinegar
10g caster sugar (it dissolves quicker than granulated)

4 large ripe tomatoes
8 strawberries, or mixed regular and wild strawberries, if you can find them

10 mint leaves
sea salt

First of all you need to prepare the dressing, as this gives the sugar time to dissolve, which tones down the acidity of the vinegar. Pour the olive oil into a non-metallic bowl, add the vinegar and sugar, give it a stir and set aside to allow the sugar time to dissolve.

Cut each tomato into 6 wedges, then cut out the seeds and discard them. Put the tomatoes into a mixing bowl.

Remove the stalks from the strawberries and slice through the tops into quarters, then add to the bowl with the tomatoes. Slice the mint leaves finely to make little green strands and add them to the bowl.

If you are serving immediately, dress the salad with the dressing, sprinkle with sea salt and serve. If you are not serving immediately, keep the dressing and sea salt separate and dress the salad just before you serve it; this will stop the salad becoming mushy.

Fruity carrot coleslaw

We use dried rather than fresh fruit in this coleslaw because, if you add apple or orange, they tend to become soft and mushy as they sit in the mayonnaise. The dried fruit also gives individual hits of sweetness as you eat it... and you probably have some dried fruit in the cupboard, so it's always handy. We have given a recipe for mayonnaise, but you can use shop-bought if you are short of time. For the home-made version, use eggs at room temperature, as this can help the mayonnaise come together more easily. This mix will give a little too much mayonnaise, but trying to make it with just one egg yolk is tricky. Some people add mustard to their mayonnaise, but we find that can be a bit harsh with the coleslaw for this recipe.

SERVES 4

2 tsp white wine vinegar
2 egg yolks (keep the whites for another recipe, perhaps Meringues, see page 207)

250ml sunflower oil (poured into a jug)
sea salt and freshly ground black pepper
½ small white cabbage (the hard white ones are best for crispness)

2 spring onions
1 large carrot, peeled and coarsely grated
80g dried fruit, such as sultanas, raisins, or even some mixed peel, or a mix of all the above

Warm the vinegar in the microwave for literally 2 seconds (you just want to take the chill off it) or warm it very gently over the lowest possible heat in a small saucepan. Drop the egg yolks into a blender and blend on high for 10 seconds, then, with the motor running, drizzle in a touch of the vinegar to warm the yolks, then one-quarter of the oil. Now add the rest of the vinegar followed by the rest of the oil, remembering to keep the flow of the oil slow and the motor fast. Season, then refrigerate.

Next take a chopping board and a sharp knife and cut the half cabbage in half. Lay each piece on its curved side, cut out the core and discard. Then shred the cabbage – the finer the better.

Slice off the coarse green ends and roots of the spring onions, then wash and chop finely.

Put the cabbage, carrot and spring onions in a bowl with the dried fruit and mix in enough mayonnaise to bind. Season and refrigerate.

If the coleslaw is not needed immediately you can leave the prepared vegetables in the fridge – unmixed with the mayonnaise – until required. Chilling the prepared vegetables will also ensure that they are nice and crisp.

Courgette, marjoram and toasted almond salad

This combination of soft courgette and crunchy almonds makes a great side salad. Try adding a little English feta (see page 67) and some granary bread croutons to turn it into a meal. If you cannot get hold of marjoram – and it can be tricky – try oregano instead. If you can't get hold of either you can use dried; there is obviously a difference but next time you find the fresh herb you could try the recipe again and check out the flavour yourself. In this recipe you will see that you are asked to smash the herbs with the sugar, this is because the sugar acts as an abrasive and helps to break them up.

You can use the ribboning trick we employ here on other vegetables: try it with asparagus or carrots – it changes the look of your salad and makes an interesting textural difference.

SERVES 4

small bunch of marjoram (or oregano)
½ tsp granulated sugar
50ml sunflower oil
2 tbsp white wine vinegar
100g whole blanched almonds
3 medium courgettes
sea salt and freshly ground black pepper

Pick the leaves from the marjoram and pop
them into a small bowl (or, better still, a mortar).

Add the sugar and, using the end of a rolling pin
(or a pestle), smash the sugar and marjoram just
a little, to break the leaves and release the oils.
Tip it into a mixing bowl, unless you were using
one of those already, in which case leave it there.

Pour in the oil and vinegar and mix. Allow to
sit and infuse while you finish the recipe.

Heat a dry frying pan until fairly hot (not too hot
or some burning will happen). Add the almonds
and, using a wooden spoon, stir continually so
they don't catch. Once they are golden, tip them
out on to a plate to prevent them overcooking.

Wash the courgettes, then trim off the top and
bottom. If you have a swivelly peeler, the next
bit will be easy; if you have a regular peeler it is
fine but just a bit trickier. Lay the courgette flat
and, using your peeler, slide it from one end to
the other along the length so that you have long
strips. When you hit the seeds in the centre, stop,
turn the courgette over and repeat on the other
side. You should have lots of 'ribbons'. It may
seem like a lot at first, but they will soon flop.

Put the courgettes and almonds in a large pretty
serving bowl, season well and add the dressing,
then carefully mix so you don't break the ribbons.

Heritage potato salad with truffled mayonnaise

A trendy version of good old potato salad. Heritage potatoes are actually varieties which were commonplace before the Second World War. To feed the country, new types of potato were introduced which were easier to grow and gave a higher yield. When the war was over, the new varieties stayed and their predecessors disappeared. Various companies have now reintroduced the old spuds and you can find them in good supermarkets and at farmer's markets. You can also find truffle oil in most supermarkets; drizzle it on soups, salads or use it in Truffled mushroom and dill pâté (see page 89). This recipe calls for shop-bought mayonnaise, as making such a small amount is difficult, but there is a recipe on page 78 if you want to make your own. This salad would make good friends with Heritage tomatoes and Yorkshire Fettle on toast (see page 67).

If your potatoes ever do that thing where they overcook and burst open, don't worry, just drain them, sprinkle with olive oil, herbs and sea salt and bake in a hot oven until crispy. Eat them for lunch, then start again on the salad. Waste not want not.

SERVES 4

500g heritage potatoes (Pink Fir Apple, Salad Blue and Dunbar Rover are a few examples)

sea salt and freshly ground black pepper
2 tbsp white truffle oil
160g shop-bought mayonnaise
3 spring onions, finely chopped

Put the potatoes in a pan, cover with water, add a good shake of salt and simmer until cooked. Be careful; heritage potatoes can be temperamental, and sometimes they turn from raw to utter mush in a minute. Pierce with a knife and, as soon as the centre is soft and there is no resistance, drain and run under cold water to prevent overcooking.

While the potatoes cool, mix the truffle oil into the mayonnaise, then fold in most of the spring onions. Although the mayonnaise is already seasoned, add a little more seasoning, as you have to compensate for the fact that it will be divided between the potatoes.

When the potatoes are cooled (they must be cold, otherwise they will break up), slice them into equal-sized pieces and dress with the mayonnaise, sprinkling with the reserved spring onions.

Chive egg mayonnaise sandwich

We love taking classics and twisting them. This is a simple and traditional filling, but the chives infused into the oil help to cut the richness of the mayonnaise, giving balance and getting the maximum amount of flavour to lift the simple sandwich to a new level; it also gives a better colour. When making mayonnaise, leave the eggs out of the fridge for a few hours; it works better when they are not cold. Warming the vinegar, as is mentioned in the recipe, helps to prevent splitting. Use a blender to make mayonnaise – it's much quicker than a hand whisk.

SERVES 6

For the mayonnaise
> small bunch of chives
> 250ml sunflower oil (poured into a jug)
> 2 egg yolks (keep the whites for Meringues, see page 207)
>
> 2 tsp white wine vinegar
> sea salt and freshly ground black pepper

For the sandwiches
> 8 medium eggs
> a loaf of your favourite bread
> some watercress, or another leaf if
> you prefer

Make your mayonnaise first, as this will help to develop the flavours. Set up a blender and, using a pair of scissors, snip the chives into the blender bowl.

Add 100ml of oil and blend the mixture for 30 seconds. Use a rubber spatula to remove all the chive oil into a separate bowl. The longer you can leave this the better; lots of flavour is being released right now.

Now wash and dry the blender bowl – this may seem strange, as you are going to make the rest of the mayonnaise in it, but the chives release water that can affect the mayonnaise, causing it to split.

Make the mayonnaise with the egg yolks, vinegar and remaining oil exactly as on page 78. Turn the blender off. Pass the chive oil through a fine sieve to remove the herbs and catch it in the jug you used for the sunflower oil (saving washing up again).

Now you have to be careful, as the chive oil contains some water from the chives and this could spoil the mayonnaise.

Season the mayonnaise, then turn the motor on full, drizzle in the chive oil and, as soon as it is incorporated, immediately turn the blender off. Transfer to a mixing bowl and chill. The mayonnaise, not you.

Now on to the sandwiches. Take the eggs, put in a saucepan, cover with cold water and cook for 12 minutes (medium eggs cooked for 12 minutes will be hard-boiled, a good thing to remember). When they are cooked, drain off the hot water, rattle the eggs around to break their shells, then cover with cold water. Let them sit for 5–10 minutes to fully cool; the cold water will get into the cracks and make peeling easier. When fully cooled, peel and chop. Add to the mayonnaise and mix. Taste it – you will want to eat it before it even hits the bread.

Slice your bread, add the egg mayonnaise, then your choice of leaves and finally the lid.

There are so many variations to this. One unusual but great one is to get a bag of your favourite crisps, sprinkle them on to the egg mayonnaise and then add the lid; you will be pleasantly surprised. Or, instead of chives in the mayonnaise, try making it with 1 tsp mild curry powder instead.

Truffled mushroom and dill pâté sandwich

This recipe started life as something called mushroom *duxelles*, a French recipe which is part of the classic beef Wellington. Ironically, we have transformed it into a vegan recipe. Adding the dill helps to balance the richness of the truffley mushrooms and creates something quite intriguing. You can find truffle oil in most supermarkets now; it's expensive but you won't use much, as it is quite strong. You can use it to drizzle on soups and salads as well. If you want to get people's attention, add it to hot soup at the table, as the aroma carried from the steaming soup will fill a room.

This pâté is a useful little recipe – you can serve it warm on toast, add whole cooked mushrooms and use it as a pie filling, or even serve it with a salad as a starter at a dinner party. On and on and on…

***

SERVES 6

400g flat mushrooms
a little sunflower oil
1 medium onion, finely chopped
25ml red wine
small bunch of dill, coarse stalks removed,
fronds chopped

white truffle oil
sea salt and freshly ground black pepper
bread and salad leaves of your choice

Wipe the mushrooms, or peel them if they look very dirty. You can wash them if you prefer, but you will find that they absorb water and that will impair the flavour. Put the mushrooms in a blender and pulse until they are smooth, but try to leave a little texture.

Pour a little sunflower oil into a large saucepan and add the onion. The wider the pan the better, as it allows the mushrooms to dry out quicker. Allow the onion to soften, then tip in all the mushrooms and add the red wine.

Cook for about 25 minutes over a medium heat, stirring occasionally to prevent sticking. Basically you are trying to evaporate the juices to get a firm, dry result. The best way to tell if it's done is by running your wooden spoon along the base of the pan; if any juice runs into the gap, cook for longer until it is completely dry.

While the mix is still hot, add the dill and truffle oil and season to taste. Allow to cool completely.

When cold, spread on to a slice of bread, add salad leaves and close the sandwich.

Tomato, basil and spring onion pâté sandwich

You could cheat and use canned beans here (drained and rinsed) but this recipe calls for dried beans; it will give you a sense of achievement. You will, however, need to soak the beans overnight in cold water.

You can take this pâté up a level by shaping it on to a plate with Courgette, marjoram and toasted almond salad (see page 82) and serving as a starter.

SERVES 6

200g dried haricot beans, soaked in plenty of water overnight

4 spring onions
about 12 basil leaves
150g tomato purée
sea salt and freshly ground black pepper

bread and salad leaves of your choice (Iceberg is good here, as it has a crunch)

Drain the beans from their soaking water, put into a saucepan, cover with water, bring to a boil, then simmer for 30–40 minutes. Check the beans to make sure they are soft. When they are cooked, drain, put in a bowl and add lots of cold water to cool them down and arrest the cooking.

When they have completely cooled down, sit the beans in a colander to drain. Leave them there while you prepare the other ingredients, to make sure they are well drained.

Cut off the roots from the spring onions, then a couple of centimetres from the green tops. Wash, drain and chop very finely.

Chop the basil leaves finely.

Put the beans in a blender and blend until smooth, then transfer to a mixing bowl and fold in the spring onions, basil and tomato purée. Season with salt and lots of pepper.

Spread the pâté on to your favourite bread, top with leaves and close the sandwich.

Cheddar and sage scones

The combination of mature Cheddar and sage works beautifully here, and is best complemented by home-made Apple chutney (see page 107). Here we use a mixture of butter and sunflower oil, which helps keep the scones moist. For light and fluffy scones, handle the dough gently, and ensure you preheat the oven well in advance so they cook quickly and don't dry out. Try to get the strongest Cheddar you can; it does make a difference to the flavour.

MAKES 8 LARGE SCONES

50g cold unsalted butter, chopped
400g self-raising flour, plus more
to dust

4 tbsp English mustard powder
2 tbsp granulated sugar
2 tsp sea salt
300g mature Cheddar cheese, grated
3 eggs
60–75ml whole milk, plus more
to glaze

10g sage leaves
50g sunflower oil

Preheat the oven to 170°C/fan 150°C/ gas mark 3½.

Rub the butter into the flour, mustard powder, sugar and salt in a large mixing bowl, until you have a texture like crumbs. Add the Cheddar, mix and make a well in the centre.

Crack the eggs into a measuring jug and top up to 225ml with milk, then add the sage and oil. Blitz together using a hand-held blender. Pour into the well in the dry ingredients and mix, gradually incorporating the flour mixture to form a dough. Be gentle.

Roll the dough out carefully on a lightly floured worktop, using a floured rolling pin, to 2cm thick, trying to keep a 20cm square shape. Using a floured knife, cut into four squares, then cut each square diagonally in half to make eight triangle-shaped scones.

Place gently on a baking tray lined with baking parchment and brush the tops with a little milk. Bake for 12–15 minutes or until risen and a light golden brown. You may need to turn the tray around halfway through to ensure they cook evenly in the oven.

Transfer carefully to a wire rack with a palette knife, leave for 10 minutes, then serve while still warm, with chutney.

Scotch duck egg with tomato jam

This is a really interesting dish. As it has a meaty feel to it, the sweet and sour of the tomato jam makes a good complement. You can serve these hot straight away, or allow to cool, chill and serve with a salad, or take to work for lunch. Try omitting the sage and replacing with 1 tsp of good curry powder instead, for a very different result.

If you can't get hold of duck's eggs, use regular hen's eggs, or even quail's eggs. The latter make for a fiddlier dish to put together, but the results look amazing scattered on a little salad. And, of course, if you use different eggs, the cooking time will vary both for boiling the eggs and deep-frying the coated Scotch eggs.

MAKES 4

For the Scotch eggs
    4 duck's eggs
    1 medium onion, finely chopped
    6 sage leaves, finely chopped
    45g sunflower oil, plus more
    to deep-fry

    4 medium hen's eggs, lightly beaten
    225g breadcrumbs
    sea salt and freshly ground
    black pepper
    Tomato jam (see page 105), to serve

To coat
    plain flour, to dust
    1 egg, lightly beaten with a little milk
    breadcrumbs, to coat

Bring enough water to the boil in a saucepan to cover the duck's eggs. Using a spoon, carefully add the duck's eggs and simmer for 9 minutes. Drain and run cold water over them until completely cold, to prevent overcooking. Shake the eggs around the pan to break the shell, cover in cold water and let them sit for 5 to 10 minutes – the water will get under the shell and make them easier to peel.

As you wait for the eggs to cool, get a bowl and add the onion, sage, sunflower oil, beaten eggs and the breadcrumbs, then season and give it a very good mix. It will seem wet but, as the breadcrumbs soak up the egg, it should become in consistency like a kind of clay (pottery skills not essential).

Peel the duck's eggs, then dry them on kitchen paper. Take one-quarter of the onion mix and, with both hands, shape it around an egg. Try to make sure it is even and especially that none of the egg is exposed. Repeat to wrap all the Scotch eggs.

Wash your hands and dry them well. Put the flour for coating in a shallow dish, the egg and milk in another and the breadcrumbs in a third. Carefully roll a Scotch egg in the flour, shake off any excess, and then roll in the egg. Finally, carefully roll in the breadcrumbs. The trickiest thing is to make sure the eggs are coated, but not so much that there are lumps all over. Repeat to coat all the eggs.

Now you can either refrigerate the eggs and fry later, or fry immediately. To do this, bring sufficient sunflower oil to 180°C/350°F, then carefully add the eggs to the oil, preferably two at a time, but no more. Use a slotted spoon to turn them so they cook evenly. When they are golden brown (it will take about 4 minutes), remove them from the oil with the slotted spoon and drain on kitchen paper. Repeat to cook the rest.

Serve immediately with the Tomato jam; maybe add a handful of your favourite salad. Or allow to cool, refrigerate and serve with leaves and Radishes with garlic milk dressing (see page 188).

Piccalilli

Piccalilli started life in India – the English brought the idea back to England and adapted it to what we know today. When you look at the ingredients, you can see the Indian influence in spices such as turmeric. A lot of recipes ask you to sprinkle the vegetables with salt and leave overnight, but this is a quick version, as I'm sure you have other things you could be doing. A trainee chef once shared her secret, which was to serve piccalilli with a spoonful of yogurt, genius when you think about it as it helps to temper the mustard and give a more mellow flavour. You will need to have some sterilised jars, which is quite easy to do: wash some jars and lids in hot soapy water and then let them dry in an oven at 140°C/fan 120°C/gas mark 1. Make sure you add the pickle to the jars while it and the jars are both still quite hot, as this creates a vacuum at the top of the jar; that's why you get a pop when you open a new jar of jam. Allocate yourself a good amount of time for this recipe, as it's a bit fiddly.

With a bit of imagination, you can twist this recipe quite easily. Try adding honey, thyme, garlic, cabbage, carrot, horseradish, celery…

MAKES 3–4 X 450G JARS

450g little pickling onions, peeled
1 large cauliflower, broken into florets
450g green beans, topped, tailed and halved
1 cucumber, halved lengthways and deseeded
2 red peppers, deseeded and cut into 2cm
(¾in) chunks

1 large head of broccoli, broken into florets
2 Granny Smith apples, peeled, cored and
cut into chunks

1 small red chilli, chopped, with its seeds
750ml white malt vinegar
180g granulated sugar, plus more if needed
4 bay leaves
1 tbsp ground cumin (see the Indian
influence coming in…)

1 tbsp ground ginger
1 tbsp turmeric
1 tbsp English mustard powder (… and
now the English touch)

3 tbsp cornflour
sea salt

You should have your vegetables, apples and chilli prepared as detailed in the ingredients list. Take a large pan, pour in the vinegar, then add the sugar and bay leaves.

Now, you are just blanching everything at this stage as you want your pickle to have a bit of a crunch at the end. Bring the vinegar to the boil and drop in the vegetables, apples and chilli (you may have to do this in two batches, depending on the size of your pan). Return the vinegar to the boil, then immediately remove the vegetables and so on with a slotted spoon and leave them on a plate or a tray to cool. They don't have to cool completely, just let them hang around.

Remove the bay leaves. Now add the spices and mustard to the vinegar. Using a balloon whisk, blend all these in, making sure there are no lumps.

Mix the cornflour in a bowl with a little water until it is runny, then return the vinegar to the boil and whisk in the cornflour well to make sure no lumps form. Let it simmer for 20 seconds to cook the cornflour, stirring occasionally to make sure it all stays smooth, then turn the heat off.

Next, return the vegetables, apples and chilli to the pan and season with salt. At this stage, taste the piccalilli, make sure it is seasoned well and, if it is too sharp for you, add a shot of sugar.

Leave the pickle to cool for 5 minutes, then carefully place in the dried-but-warm jars. As soon as the piccalilli is in the jars, screw the lids on.

Allow to cool. Some say the flavours improve with time, but you be the judge of that. You can keep it for 8 weeks in a cool, dark place.

Pickled cucumbers and gherkins in horseradish vinegar

The idea for horseradish vinegar came from Hungary – it's quite popular over there. This dish has quite a kick, so try serving it with a Red onion, vintage Cheddar and sage pasty (see page 72), or anything else which is a bit rich. This recipe will make more vinegar than you need, but it keeps well and you will want to use it again. You need to make the vinegar first and allow it to cool; if you use it while it is warm it will ruin the cucumbers. Allowing the pickles to sit in the vinegar for a couple of hours will also help to develop the flavour.

As well as being a pretty useful salad, you can add the cucumbers and gherkins to a sandwich for a bit of bite.

SERVES 4

3cm piece of horseradish, peeled
100g granulated sugar
500ml white distilled vinegar
sea salt
1 medium cucumber
4 large gherkins
small sprig of dill, finely chopped

Using a peeler, shave the horseradish into thin slices. Put half of them in a saucepan and set the rest aside; be warned, your eyes may sting.

Now add the sugar and vinegar to the saucepan with 100ml of water, season with a good pinch of salt, then bring to a simmer and keep it there for 2 minutes. Allow to cool completely. When cool, add the reserved horseradish.

Take a slice from each end of the cucumber, then slice in half lengthways. Using a teaspoon, slide it along the seeds to remove them. Then cut the cucumber into 1cm slices, preferably on an angle to add interest. Put in a mixing bowl.

Now slice the gherkins into thin slices about 5mm thick and add to the bowl with the cucumbers. Sprinkle on the dill and add enough horseradish vinegar to cover everything.

Cover and leave the pickles for a couple of hours for the flavours to develop, then serve.

PANTRY

Microwave brown sauce

This is a delicious balance of savoury and sweet. Great to have in the fridge, ready to elevate the next late-night dinner of cheese on toast to a special treat. It also makes an excellent gift as part of a hamper of good cheeses and crackers.

If you haven't got a microwave, just stick all the ingredients in a good strong pan and boil it like billy-o. I think that's how you spell billy-o...

MAKES 800ML

650g (about 4) Braeburn apples, peeled, cored and roughly chopped

300g pitted dates, chopped
100g dark brown sugar, plus more if needed

1 medium onion, roughly chopped
300ml balsamic vinegar
1 tsp ground ginger
1 tsp ground allspice
¼ tsp cayenne pepper
¼ tsp ground nutmeg
1 tbsp sea salt, plus more if needed

Mix together all the ingredients in a large, microwavable bowl or container, pour in 200ml of water and cover loosely with a plate or lid. Microwave at full power (800W) for 10–15 minutes, stirring every 5, until the apples and onions have softened.

Blend to a smooth purée using a hand-held blender, then microwave again with the lid on for a further 5–10 minutes, or until the sauce is thick and a spoonful put on a cold plate doesn't run. Taste and add more salt or sugar as needed to ensure a balance.

Allow to cool completely, then pot in a sterilised 1kg jar (see page 97). This will keep for up to a month in the fridge.

Tomato jam

Tomatoes, with all their natural sweetness and vibrancy, make an excellent jam. You can use this as an alternative to tomato ketchup, or as a filling for savoury scones and sandwiches; it's almost like a sweet chutney. It's also a great way to use up leftover tomatoes.

MAKES 700G

750g (6 large) tomatoes, roughly chopped

2 tbsp white wine vinegar
1 tbsp sea salt, plus more if needed
250g caster sugar, plus more if needed
2 tsp tomato purée

Place the tomatoes, vinegar and salt in a large, microwavable bowl or container, covering loosely with a plate or lid. Microwave at full power (800W) for 10–15 minutes, stirring every 5, until the tomatoes are very soft.

Add the sugar and tomato purée, then blitz to a smooth consistency with a hand-held blender.

Return to the microwave without the lid for a further 25–30 minutes, stirring every 5, until thick and a spoonful put on a chilled plate doesn't run. You may think this is a long time, but it's a lot quicker than it would be on the hob. You need it to cook this long to reduce the water content that was in the tomatoes. Taste and add more salt or sugar if necessary. Allow to cool.

(If you haven't got a microwave, put everything in a heavy-based pan, cover and cook for 5 minutes. Remove the lid and cook, stirring, until thick and a spoonful put on a chilled plate doesn't run. If the jam sticks to the pan a bit don't worry, as this helps the flavour. Whizz with a hand-held blender for a more jammy texture.)

Pot in a 600ml (or two smaller) sterilised jar(s) (see page 97), while it and the jars are still warm. It keeps for a month in the fridge.

Red onion chutney

Again, this is very simple and quick to prepare because it's cooked in the microwave, which preserves the vibrant colour and flavour of the onions. Serve it as part of a ploughman's lunch, on a grilled cheese sandwich, or with a nice bit of Summer quiche (see page 150).

─────────

MAKES 685G

1kg (about 6) red onions, thinly sliced
juice of 2 lemons
2 tbsp sea salt, plus more if needed
150g granulated sugar, plus more
if needed

Place the onions, lemon juice and salt in a large, microwavable bowl or container and cover loosely with a plate or lid. Microwave at full power (800W) for 10 minutes, stirring every 5.

Mix in the sugar, then return to the microwave with the lid on for another 15–20 minutes, again stirring every 5 minutes. It needs this long to reduce the moisture, and it's still a lot less time than it would take on the hob.

The chutney is ready once most of the liquid has evaporated and the colour has changed to a deep purple. If you put a spoonful of the chutney on a chilled plate it should hold its shape and shouldn't run. Taste and add more salt or sugar if necessary. Allow to cool.

(If you haven't got a microwave, put all the ingredients in a heavy-based pan, cover and cook for 5 minutes to allow the juices to leach from the onions; they will cook in this juice, for more flavour. Remove the lid and continue to cook until the onions are very well cooked and sticky. If the chutney sticks to the pan a bit don't worry, as this helps with the flavour.)

Pot in a 500ml sterilised jar (see page 97), while it and the jar are still warm. It will keep for a month in the fridge.

Apple chutney

An essential, this goes with almost anything. We use Braeburn apples, which have a good balance of acidity and sweetness, but feel free to experiment with different varieties such as Cox's, Bramley or russet, which will each lend their particular character to your chutney. Using the microwave to make the chutney saves a lot of pan scraping and time as well; an Italian chef who worked with us showed us this little trick.

MAKES 1.1KG

1.5kg (about 7) Braeburn apples, peeled, cored and roughly chopped

8 tbsp (60ml) cider vinegar
2 tbsp sea salt, plus more if needed
200g granulated sugar, plus more if needed

Place the apples, vinegar and salt in a large, microwavable bowl or container, covering loosely with a plate or lid. Microwave at full power (800W) for 10–15 minutes, stirring every 5, until the apples are soft and plump.

Add the sugar. Pulse with a hand-held blender to a chunky consistency, then return the chutney to the microwave, uncovered, for a further 5 to 10 minutes, mixing every 5, or until thick and a spoonful put on a cold surface doesn't run.

Taste and add more salt or sugar if necessary. Allow to cool.

(If you haven't got a microwave, put all the ingredients in a heavy-based pan and bring to the boil, then reduce the heat to a fast simmer. When the fruit is pulpy, use a balloon whisk to smash up the fruit, but leave some for texture. Allow another 20 minutes' cooking time, then test by putting a little on a chilled plate; allow to cool, then check for consistency.)

Sterilise four 227ml jam jars (see page 97). Divide the chutney between them while both it and the jars are still warm. This will keep for up to a month in the fridge.

Fried onion vinaigrette

Perfect with the more peppery, bitter salad leaves such as watercress or radicchio, this is best made the day before using, so the flavour has time to infuse the oil properly.

MAKES 300ML

1 large onion, finely chopped
300ml sunflower oil
pinch of sea salt
2 tbsp sherry vinegar

Using a large, heavy-based frying pan, or a casserole dish, gently fry the onion in 2 tbsp of the oil with the salt.

Once the onion is golden brown and soft enough that, when squeezed between your thumb and forefinger, there is no resistance, add the rest of the oil and heat gently. Once all the oil has warmed through, remove from the heat and allow to cool completely. Add a little more salt and the sherry vinegar.

Pulse to a chunky vinaigrette using a hand-held blender, then check for seasoning. Cover and leave the oil to infuse for a minimum of 1 hour, but preferably overnight, before serving.

Basic shortcrust pastry

This is a simple shortcrust. The savoury version can be used for pies and quiches; the sweet makes a great base for tarts. The trick is in rolling out the pastry between two sheets of baking parchment – this way you don't need to use any extra flour so the mix stays buttery and moist.

The pastry can be made the night before and kept in the fridge. If you're using it to line a tart case, just be sure to take it out a good 30 minutes before you need to use it, so it has time to soften.

You can add 10g finely chopped herbs, or 1 tbsp finely grated unwaxed lemon zest, to add a different flavour to the pastry.

MAKES ENOUGH TO LINE
A 20CM TART TIN

For savoury pastry
250g plain flour
pinch of sea salt
125g cold unsalted butter, chopped
about 6 tbsp water

For sweet pastry
150g plain flour
50g granulated sugar
pinch of sea salt
100g cold unsalted butter, chopped
about 4 tbsp water

Set up a food processor fitted with the blade attachment and add the flour, sugar (if making sweet pastry), salt and butter. Pulse the mix to form a consistency like fine crumbs, ensuring the butter is incorporated. Or place the flour, sugar (if making sweet pastry) and salt in a large bowl and rub in the butter with your fingertips untl it looks like fine crumbs.

Let the processor run continuously while slowly pouring the water down the funnel until the mix comes together to form a ball of dough, or just mix it in with the blade of a butter knife. You may not need all the water, so go carefully; similarly you may need to add a little more if it doesn't come together. Once the dough has formed, turn off the machine, or stop mixing with the knife; it will be difficult to roll out (and the pastry will be tougher) if overworked.

Place the pastry between sheets of baking parchment. Using a rolling pin, roll out to a thickness of 2mm. Try to ensure the dough is level and even.

At this stage you can use the pastry straight away or keep it in the fridge for up to 5 days, stored flat on a tray and covered tightly with cling film.

Strawberry and vanilla butter

Adding fruit to butter is a simple yet effective way to incorporate variety and flavour into your cooking. The possibilities are endless. Lemon, lime or orange zests (make sure they are unwaxed) work great, or, for a savoury version, try smoked sea salt or crushed peppercorns (obviously omit the sugar!). Whatever you choose to add, make sure to use the best quality unsalted butter you can afford. Spread the sweet butters thickly over toast and scones, and use the savoury varieties on jacket potatoes and greens.

MAKES 275G

200g unsalted butter, softened
2 tbsp icing sugar, sifted
½ vanilla pod, split, seeds scraped out
75g (about 4) strawberries, hulled and finely chopped

Beat the butter, sugar and vanilla seeds for 5 minutes in a large bowl using a wooden spoon, or in a food mixer with the beater attachment. Add the berries and beat to combine.

Use immediately, or cover and set in a small mould or dish in the fridge until required.

Lemon curd

This makes a great gift and can be prepared well in advance and kept in the fridge. We have tried using other fruit juices for this, such as lime and passion fruit, and they both work really well. It's best spread on hot buttered toast or served with our White chocolate, apricot and coconut scones (see page 124).

MAKES 600ML

finely grated zest and juice of
5 unwaxed lemons

5 eggs, lightly beaten
175g unsalted butter, chopped
375g granulated sugar

Combine all the ingredients in a large heatproof bowl. Create a bain-marie: place the bowl over a saucepan one-third full of gently simmering water, making sure the water does not touch the bowl, as this will overheat the curd.

Keeping the heat low, whisk to incorporate the butter as it melts. Once the butter is combined you can just whisk every 10 minutes or so, using a spatula to scrape the sides of the bowl clean (any mix left here will overcook).

After 45 minutes to 1 hour the curd will have thickened and you can test to see if it's ready by putting a little on a chilled plate: if it holds its shape, it is ready. Pass through a sieve to remove the zest and any lumps.

Divide between two 340ml sterilised jam jars (see page 97) while both curd and jars are still hot. Allow to cool before serving. This will keep for up to 1 month in the fridge.

Microwave pear jam

By cooking this in the microwave you not only reduce the cooking time, but preserve the real flavour and colour of the fruit. The risk of burning the base of the pan also disappears!

We've chosen pears here, but you can use whatever fruit you like: apples, strawberries and rhubarb all work beautifully. Just be aware you may have to adjust the amount of sugar and the cooking time depending on the acidity and water content of the fruit.

MAKES 1.5KG

1.5kg (about 8) Conference pears, peeled, cored and chopped

juice of 1 lemon
250g white caster sugar

Place the fruit and lemon juice in a large, microwavable bowl or container, covering loosely with a plate or lid. Microwave at full power (800W) for 10 minutes, stirring after 5.

Add the sugar and pulse the mix with a hand-held blender, but keep it chunky: it's better to have pieces of fruit than perfect smoothness.

Return to the microwave, uncovered, for a final 15–20 minutes or until the water from the fruit has mostly evaporated, mixing every 5 minutes. It needs this long because there's a lot of moisture in the pears that needs to be evaporated. Test to see if the jam is ready by putting a little on a chilled plate: if it holds its shape, it's ready. Allow to cool completely.

(If you haven't got a microwave, put all the ingredients into a pan and bring to the boil, then reduce the heat until it is at a fast simmer. After 10 minutes – or when the fruit is pulpy – use a balloon whisk to smash up the fruit, but leave some texture. Allow 20 minutes' more cooking time, then test by putting a little on a chilled plate, and checking if it holds its shape. Cook for a little longer if needed before testing again.)

Pot into sterilised jars (see page 97) while it and the jars are still warm. It will keep for a month in the fridge.

Sweet pesto

This may sound a little strange, but it is delicious and adds instant flavour and colour to any variety of dishes. Try serving it on our Best porridge (see page 14), or dribble a little on a sponge cake with some cream. You can experiment with different herbs, such as lemon thyme or tarragon.

MAKES 600ML

50g flaked almonds
5 tbsp sunflower oil
pinch of sea salt
15g bunch of mint
1 tbsp icing sugar, sifted

Preheat the oven to 160°C/fan 140°C/gas mark 3.

Spread the flaked almonds over a baking tray and place in the oven to toast for 15–20 minutes until golden brown, turning with a spatula after 10 minutes to ensure they brown evenly.

Using a food processor or hand-held blender, blitz the almonds, oil and salt to form a nutty paste.

Pick the mint leaves and add them with the icing sugar. Blitz again until smooth.

This can be kept in an airtight container in the fridge for up to a week.

Salted butterscotch

This balance of sweet and salty is as irresistible as it is versatile. Use it as a filling for cakes and biscuits, or with ice cream for a quick dessert, or just eat it out of the jar with a spoon! Be warned: this gets very hot when it is cooking, so don't be tempted to have a quick taste.

MAKES 600G

250g granulated sugar
350ml double cream
100g unsalted butter, chopped
½ tsp sea salt, plus more if needed

Place the sugar in the biggest, heaviest-based pan you have, making sure the pan is very clean and very dry. Heat gently over a low heat until all the sugar has dissolved and turned into a golden brown caramel. Avoid stirring, as this increases the chance of the caramel crystallising. If you see that one part of the pan is hotter than the rest, turn it around so it cooks evenly. Bring the cream to the boil in another heavy-based saucepan.

Once all the sugar has caramelised, pour in the cream. Be careful, as the sugar is now very hot and the cream will bubble up and spit. Once it has settled down, increase the heat to medium. With a wooden spoon, stir in the cream and cook until thick and a deep golden brown, which will take 2 to 5 minutes.

Test if the butterscotch is ready by putting a little of the mix on a chilled plate. It should hold its shape; if not, keep it bubbling away for a couple more minutes, then test again.

Remove from the pan from the heat and whisk in the butter and salt. Pass through a fine metal sieve into a clean and dry heatproof bowl. Taste and add more salt if necessary.

You can use this straight away, or leave to cool, then cover and set in the fridge overnight.

Toasted marzipan custard

If you haven't made custard from scratch before, now is your chance. It takes
a bit of time and skill, but you will be pleased with yourself at the end. This recipe
takes custard to a new higher level by infusing the liquid with toasted marzipan,
which gives it an amazing roasted almond / marzipan depth. Serve it with a sponge,
Little cherry Bakewell tarts (see page 201), or even add it to a trifle.

SERVES 4–6

unsalted butter, for the tray
150g marzipan, torn roughly into
small pieces

400ml whole milk
200ml double cream
6 egg yolks (save the whites to make
Meringues, see page 207)

25g granulated sugar
1 tbsp cornflour, sifted

Preheat the oven to 165°C/fan 145°F/gas mark 3.
Butter a baking tray, line with baking parchment
and spread over the marzipan. Toast in the
oven for 10–12 minutes, or until golden brown.

Once toasted, put the marzipan in a saucepan
with the milk and cream and bring to the boil
over a medium heat. Blitz together using a
hand-held blender; be careful, as it will be hot.
Allow the creamy mixture to infuse for at least
1 hour, but preferably overnight, in the fridge.

Pass through a fine sieve, discarding any lumps
of marzipan, then return to the boil.

In a large bowl, whisk the egg yolks, sugar and
cornflour, then pour half the hot marzipan milk
over it, whisking as you go. (Doing it this way
will reduce the risk of the egg overcooking.)
Return the mix to the remaining marzipan milk,
whisking continuously over a low heat until
thickened and you can see steam rising from the
surface; about 5 to 10 minutes should do it.
Be patient and don't let the custard boil or it
will split.

(If your custard has split, here's how to save it.
Remove the pan quickly from the heat, placing
the base in a bowl of iced water, and blitz
the contents with a hand-held blender. Pass the
custard through a sieve to remove any
overcooked egg.)

Pass once more through a fine sieve to ensure a
smooth, lump-free custard.

AFTERNOON TEA

Sally Lunn buns

As the story goes, Solange Luyon (or Sally Lunn from an English tongue) was a young French Huguenot refugee who fled to Bath in the late 17th century and began baking the brioche-like buns that became her namesake. They're very delicious and should be eaten the day they're baked, served with Strawberry and vanilla butter (see page 111), or your favourite jam. Any left over should be frozen that same day, as soon as they are cold. When defrosted, cut them open, toast and serve with scrambled eggs for a posh breakfast. It's really good.

MAKES 12

450g plain flour, plus more if needed
pinch of sea salt
75g granulated sugar
300ml single cream
2 eggs, lightly beaten, plus 1 more to glaze
10.5g (3 tsp or 1½ packets) fast-action dried yeast
finely grated zest of 1 unwaxed lemon
icing sugar, to dust

Sift the flour and salt into a large mixing bowl, stir in the sugar, then make a well in the middle.

Whisk together the cream, eggs and yeast, then add to the well in the dry ingredients along with the lemon zest. Mix with your hands to form a dough. You may need to add a little more flour if the dough is very wet. Cover with cling film and leave to prove in a warm, draught-free place for 10 minutes.

Using your hands, knead the dough for about 5 minutes (or use a food mixer fitted with the dough hook attachment), as this will help create a light, fluffy texture. Then divide the dough equally between 12 muffin moulds. Brush each bun with a little beaten egg. Cover loosely with cling film and prove for a further 20 minutes or until risen by one-third in size. Preheat the oven to 170°C/fan 150°C/gas mark 3½.

Remove the cling film and bake the buns for 10–12 minutes; they should be golden brown. Dust with icing sugar and serve warm.

White chocolate, apricot and coconut scones

Scone-making requires a gentle touch. Any heavy handling will result in flat, dense scones, because it risks overworking the protein (gluten) in the flour and that makes the scones tougher.

Don't be a slave to this recipe; if you want to use dark chocolate, or to change the fruit, then go ahead and do so.

MAKES 10

50g desiccated coconut
400g self-raising flour, sifted, plus more to dust

pinch of sea salt
150g granulated sugar
50g cold unsalted butter, chopped
100ml sunflower oil
150g white chocolate, chopped
100g dried apricots, chopped
4 eggs
10–25ml whole milk, plus more to glaze

Preheat the oven to 160°C/fan 140°C/
gas mark 3.

Spread the desiccated coconut on a baking
tray and toast in the oven for 15–20 minutes,
or until golden brown, turning it with a
spatula every 5 minutes so it cooks evenly.
Allow to cool.

Now increase the oven temperature to 170°C/
fan 150°C/gas mark 3½.

Sift the flour and salt into a large mixing bowl
and stir in the sugar. Rub the butter into the
flour mixture to form a texture like crumbs,
then stir in half the oil. Add the white chocolate,
apricots and coconut, mix and make a well in
the centre.

Crack the eggs into a measuring jug, top
up to 225ml with milk and beat together
lightly with the remaining oil. Pour into the
well and mix, gradually incorporating the
dry ingredients to form a dough. Be gentle.

Roll the dough out carefully on a lightly
floured worktop, using a floured rolling pin,
to 2cm thick, then cut out scones with a
floured 8cm pastry cutter.

Place the scones gently on to a baking tray
lined with baking parchment and brush the
tops with a little milk, then bake for 12–15
minutes or until risen and golden brown.

Transfer to a wire rack with a palette knife and
leave to cool for 10 minutes, then serve while
they still have a breath of the oven about them.

Parsnip cake with Horlicks icing and toasted hazelnuts

Parsnips may seem an odd ingredient for a cake but, if you think about it, they are actually quite sweet; we don't bat an eyelid at carrots in a cake. We pair parsnips here with malty Horlicks and toasted hazelnuts. You could add a more formal touch by serving the un-iced cake as a pudding, with a little vanilla ice cream and a few orange segments.

SERVES 6–8

For the cake
150g sunflower oil, plus more for the tin

75g ground almonds
3 eggs, lightly beaten
150g light muscovado sugar
75g self-raising flour
½ tsp baking powder
¼ tsp ground ginger
pinch of sea salt
150g (1 medium) parsnip, peeled and grated

For the icing
125g unsalted butter, softened
125g icing sugar, sifted
50g Horlicks malted milk drink

To decorate
50g hazelnuts, skinned
icing sugar, to dust (optional)

Preheat the oven to 155°C/fan 135°F/gas mark 3. Oil a 26 x 12cm loaf tin and line the base with baking parchment.

Spread the ground almonds and hazelnuts (for decoration later) on separate baking trays, then toast in the oven for 15–20 minutes, or until golden brown, turning them with a spatula every 5 minutes so they cook evenly. The hazelnuts may take a little longer. Set aside to cool.

For the cake, whisk the eggs, oil and sugar in a large mixing bowl (or use a food mixer fitted with the beater attachment), then add the flour, ground almonds, baking powder, ginger and salt. Lastly fold in the parsnip and mix thoroughly.

Spoon into the prepared tin and bake for 45–50 minutes, or until firm to the touch and a skewer inserted into the middle of the cake comes out clean. Allow to cool in the tin for 10 minutes, then turn out on to a wire rack.

While the cake cools, make the icing by beating the butter and icing sugar in a large mixing bowl until light and fluffy (or use a food mixer fitted with the beater attachment). Make a paste with the Horlicks and 2 tbsp of boiling water, then beat this into the buttercream.

Once the cake is cool, spread the icing generously over the top, then chop the toasted hazelnuts in half and scatter over. Finish with a light dusting of icing sugar, if you like.

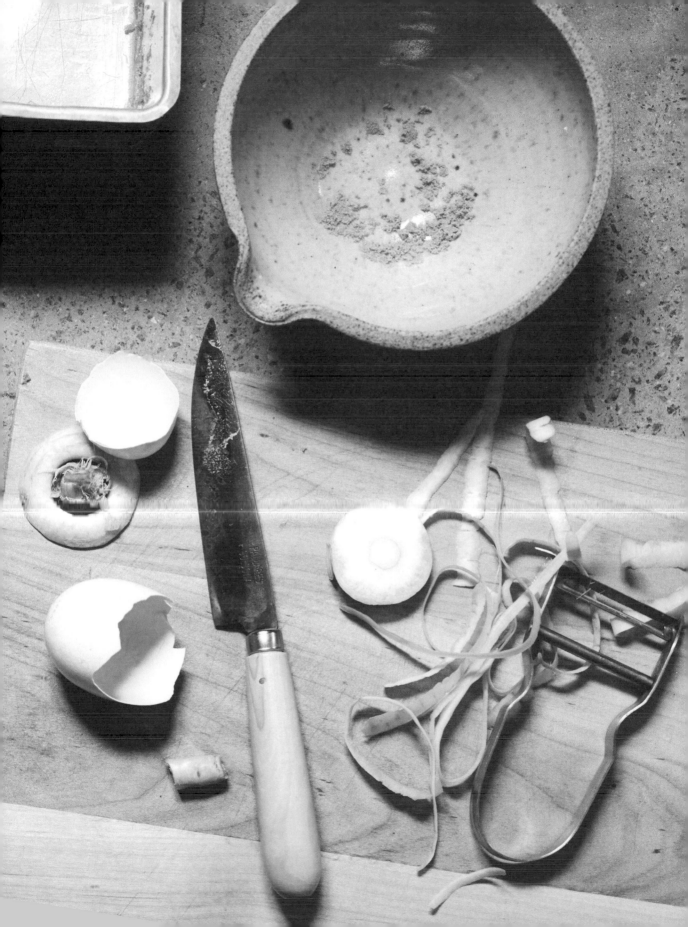

Best carrot cake with blood orange icing

Using sunflower oil instead of butter gives a wonderful moist fluffiness
to cakes and lets the flavour of the other ingredients do the talking.
We use purple carrots, which turn the cake a beautiful deep blue colour,
but, if you can't get hold of them, regular carrots work just as well.
Similarly, if it's not blood orange season, you can use regular oranges
instead. And, if you have only got one 20cm springform tin (like most
normal people), just bake the cakes one after another in the same tin.

SERVES 10–12

For the cake
  unsalted butter, for the tins
  75g walnuts
  5 eggs
  250g sunflower oil
  250g dark muscovado sugar
  250g self-raising flour
  1 tsp baking powder
  1 tsp ground cinnamon
  pinch of sea salt
  50g raisins
  50g candied mixed peel
  200g carrots (2 medium), peeled
  and grated

For the icing
  165g unsalted butter, softened
  250g full-fat cream cheese, at
  room temperature

  165g icing sugar, sifted
  finely grated zest of 2 blood oranges,
  plus 5 tbsp blood orange juice

Preheat the oven to 155°C/fan 135°C/gas mark 3. Butter two 20cm springform cake tins and line the bases with baking parchment.

Spread the walnuts on a baking tray and toast in the oven for 20–25 minutes, or until golden brown, turning them with a spatula every 5 minutes so they cook evenly. Allow to cool, then roughly chop.

To make the cake, combine the eggs, oil and sugar in a large mixing bowl using a whisk (or in a food mixer fitted with the beater attachment), then add the flour, baking powder, cinnamon and salt. Now add the raisins, mixed peel, walnuts and carrots and mix until thoroughly combined.

Divide between the prepared tins and bake for 25–30 minutes, or until firm to touch and a skewer inserted into the middle of the cakes comes out clean. Allow to cool in the tins for 10 minutes before carefully releasing from the tins and turning out on to a wire rack. (Or bake them in the same tin, one after another.)

For the icing, ensure the butter and cream cheese are at room temperature, which will reduce the risk of any lumps forming. Beat them together in a large mixing bowl (or use a food mixer fitted with the beater attachment), then add the icing sugar and beat again until thoroughly combined. Fold in half the orange zest and all the juice.

Once the cakes are cool, spread some icing in the middle, then sandwich together and generously coat the top with the rest. Decorate by sprinkling evenly with the remaining orange zest.

Pineapple and rum upside-down cake with brown butter filling

Browning the butter first gives the filling a flavour which is rather intriguing, while adding the vanilla at this browning stage produces a more pronounced taste, too. We use some spelt flour in the cake batter as it gives a delicious background nuttiness which echoes the flavour of the brown butter. If you have only got one 20cm springform tin, just bake the cakes one after another in the same tin. I think that has been said before...

SERVES 10–12

For the cake
250g sunflower oil, plus more for the tins
5 eggs, lightly beaten
250g light muscovado sugar
100g plain flour
100g spelt flour
1 tsp baking powder
pinch of sea salt
234g can of pineapple rings
6 glacé cherries

For the rum glaze
1 tbsp granulated sugar
6 tbsp dark rum

For the filling
250g unsalted butter, softened
1 vanilla pod, split, seeds scraped out
200g icing sugar, sifted

To decorate
1 punnet of edible flowers (optional)

Preheat the oven to 155°C/fan 135°C/gas mark 3. Oil two 20cm springform cake tins and line the bases with baking parchment.

For the cakes, whisk the eggs, oil and sugar in a large mixing bowl (or use a food mixer fitted with the beater attachment), then add the plain flour, spelt flour, baking powder and salt and mix until just combined.

Pat 6 pineapple rings dry with kitchen paper, then make a layer of them in the base of one of the prepared tins. If the pineapple rings are very large, you may need to slice them in half. Sit a cherry in the hole of each.

Now divide the cake batter between the two tins and bake for 35–40 minutes or until firm to the touch; a skewer should come out clean. Allow to cool in the tins for 10 minutes, then carefully release from the tins and turn out on to a wire rack, pineapple-side up. (Or bake the cakes in the same tin, one after another, adding the base layer of pineapple and cherries to just one of the cakes.)

Meanwhile, to make the glaze, simply dissolve the sugar in 2 tbsp of boiling water before adding the rum, then prick the sponges with a skewer while they're still warm and brush the glaze all over using a pastry brush.

For the filling, weigh 80g of the butter into a small, scrupulously clean saucepan with the vanilla seeds and pod and melt it over a low heat. The butter will start to sizzle and froth up; watch it closely. Once the sizzling has died down and the butter has turned a golden brown colour, a nutty aroma will be released. Immediately remove it from the heat. Allow to cool, then remove the vanilla pod.

Beat the remaining butter in a large mixing bowl (or use a stand mixer fitted with the beater attachment), then gradually beat in the cooled brown butter. Now add the icing sugar and beat again until thoroughly combined.

To assemble the cake, trim the top of the sponge without pineapples to create a flat surface, then spread on all the brown butter filling. Sit the pineapple sponge on top and scatter with edible flowers, if you like.

Coffee cake with cocoa nib icing

Cocoa nibs (see page 213) are what chocolate is made from and they will make a flavourful addition to your cooking. They are available from good chocolatiers or health food shops, although you will find that they are more reasonably priced in the latter. We know someone who used to sprinkle them on their morning muesli, which seems a very good idea.

This recipe – our nod to a mocha – uses the bitterness of cocoa nibs to complement the robust, roasted flavours of the coffee. If you can't get hold of cocoa nibs you can substitute them with a good-quality 70% cocoa solids chocolate, just shaved with a vegetable peeler and sprinkled over the top. If you have only got one 20cm springform tin, as ever with our recipes, just bake the cakes one after another in the same tin.

SERVES 10–12

For the cake
unsalted butter, for the tins
5 eggs, lightly beaten
250g sunflower oil
250g light muscovado sugar
250g self-raising flour
25g (5 heaped tbsp) instant coffee
pinch of sea salt

For the glaze
2 tbsp granulated sugar
1 tbsp instant coffee

For the cocoa nib icing
200g unsalted butter, softened
100g full-fat cream cheese, at room temperature
200g icing sugar, sifted
100g cocoa powder, sifted, plus 1 tbsp for the top (optional)
20g cocoa nibs

Preheat the oven to 155°C/fan 135°C/gas mark 3. Butter two 20cm springform cake tins and line the bases with baking parchment.

Whisk the eggs, oil and sugar in a large mixing bowl (or use a food mixer fitted with the beater attachment), then add the flour, coffee and salt. Beat until thoroughly combined.

Spoon into the prepared tins. Bake for 35–40 minutes or until firm to touch and a skewer inserted into the middle comes out clean. Allow to cool in the tins for 10 minutes before carefully releasing from the tins and turning out on to a wire rack. (Or bake them in the same tin, one after another.)

Meanwhile, make the glaze by mixing the sugar, coffee and 3 tbsp of boiling water until the sugar has dissolved. Prick the cakes all over with a skewer and brush the syrup all over with a pastry brush. This reinforces the coffee flavour and helps keep the cake moist.

For the icing, ensure your butter and cream cheese are at room temperature, which reduces the risk of lumps forming. Beat the butter and cream cheese in a large mixing bowl (or use a food mixer fitted with the beater attachment), then add the icing sugar and cocoa, beating again until thoroughly combined. Lastly fold in the cocoa nibs, reserving some for decoration.

Once the cake is cool, spread half the icing on the less attractive cake, then sandwich together and generously coat the top with the rest. Decorate with the reserved cocoa nibs and dust with the 1 tbsp of cocoa powder, if you like.

Blackberry and almond crumble cake

The crumble element in this cake is quite easy to make, as you bake it separately so that you can sprinkle it on at the end. This keeps it crunchy, as you only need to add it shortly before serving.

We use sunflower oil instead of butter for the sponge, as it gives a wonderful moist fluffiness and means the toasted almond and blackberry flavours are the focus, rather than heavier, richer butter.

SERVES 10–12

For the cake
    unsalted butter, for the tin
    125g ground almonds
    5 eggs
    250g sunflower oil
    250g golden caster sugar, plus
    25g for the purée

    125g self-raising flour
    1 tsp baking powder
    1 tsp almond extract
    pinch of sea salt
    350g blackberries

For the crumble
    50g cold unsalted butter, chopped
    75g plain flour
    25g demerara sugar
    ½ tsp ground cinnamon
    pinch of sea salt

To decorate
    50g flaked almonds
    icing sugar, to dust (optional)

Preheat the oven to 155°C/fan 135°C/gas mark 3. Butter a 23cm springform cake tin and line the base with baking parchment.

Spread the ground and flaked almonds on separate baking trays and toast for 15–20 minutes, turning them with a spatula every 5 minutes so they cook evenly, or until golden brown. Set aside to cool.

For the cake, combine the eggs, oil and the 250g of sugar in a large mixing bowl using a whisk (or mix in a food mixer fitted with the beater attachment). Whisk for several minutes, or until it turns very thick and pale (don't skip this step, or you may find that the batter tends to separate). Then add the flour, ground almonds, baking powder, almond extract and salt.

Take 75g of the blackberries, cut them in half and fold them into the batter.

Spoon into the prepared tin and bake for 55–60 minutes or until firm to touch and a skewer inserted into the middle of the cakes comes out clean.

Allow to rest in the tin for 10 minutes, then turn out on to a wire rack to cool.

Meanwhile, to make the crumble, rub the butter into the flour, sugar, cinnamon and salt in a large mixing bowl to form a texture like crumbs (or you can pulse the ingredients together in a food processor). Spread evenly over a non-stick baking tray and bake for 30–35 minutes or until golden brown, turning with a spatula every 10 minutes to ensure even cooking. Allow to cool.

To make the purée, place a small pan over a low heat. Tip in 200g of the remaining blackberries with the remaining 25g of caster sugar and 4 tbsp of water and cover the pan. Once the berries have softened (a matter of a few minutes), remove from the heat. Blend to a purée with a hand-held blender, then pass through a fine sieve to remove the seeds. Set aside to cool.

When you're ready to assemble the cake, spoon the blackberry purée over the top of the sponge, then scatter the crumble and flaked almonds all over. Finish with the remaining blackberries and dust with icing sugar, if you like. This is lovely served with a dollop of mascarpone.

Pear cakes with white chocolate icing

This recipe uses buckwheat flour, which is gluten-free (despite the deceptive name), making it a great cake for anyone with gluten intolerance. Pears have a delicate flavour, so it's best to buy them ahead of when you want to bake and let them ripen in a fruit bowl, which will enhance the taste. The white chocolate icing lends a luxuriousness, making these perfect for a birthday or special occasion. You can also make this as one big cake in a 20cm springform cake tin (you will have to bake it for longer – an extra 5–10 minutes). Next time you make this cake, try adding a handful of toasted almonds to the batter before you bake it, for a new dimension.

MAKES 16

For the cake
25g rolled oats
3 eggs, lightly beaten
125g sunflower oil
125g light muscovado sugar
100g buckwheat flour
½ tsp baking powder
pinch of sea salt
180g (1 medium) pear, cored, peeled and grated

For the white chocolate icing
100g white chocolate, plus more to serve

100g unsalted butter, softened
50g icing sugar, sifted

Preheat the oven to 155°C/fan 135°C/gas mark 3.

Toast the oats on a baking tray in the oven for 15–20 minutes, stirring occasionally, or until they begin to turn golden brown. Set aside to cool.

Whisk the eggs, oil and sugar in a large mixing bowl (or use a food mixer fitted with the beater attachment), then add the buckwheat flour, toasted oats, baking powder and salt. Now add the pear and mix until thoroughly combined.

Divide between 16 cupcake moulds and bake for 20–25 minutes or until firm to touch and a skewer inserted into the middle of the cakes comes out clean. Allow to cool in the moulds for 10 minutes before turning out on to a wire rack.

For the icing, melt the chocolate in a microwave on a low power setting, stirring often, or melt it in a heatproof bowl set over a pan of simmering water (the bowl should not touch the water). Beat the butter in a large mixing bowl (or use a food mixer fitted with the beater attachment), then add the icing sugar and beat again. Finally, fold in the melted chocolate until thoroughly combined.

Using a piping bag with a fluted nozzle, pipe the icing on to each cake, or just smooth it on thickly with a spatula or butter knife. Finish by shaving white chocolate over with a vegetable peeler.

SUPPER

Baked beetroot with home-made curds and toasted sunflower seeds

Making curds and whey is a nostalgic practice, a very basic form of cheese-making that can be done at home quite easily. You can buy vegetarian rennet online, at some supermarkets and at specialist and health food shops; some people still use it to make junket, a sweet version of curds. Oh, and of course curds were made famous by a certain Little Miss Muffet.

A nice variation to this recipe are garlic-flavoured curds: simply add a garlic clove to the milk before heating.

SERVES 4

6 golfball-sized beetroots
400ml whole milk
juice of ½ lemon
20g sea salt
40g rennet
freshly ground black pepper
50g toasted sunflower seeds
(see page 20)

Preheat the oven to 200°C/fan 180°C/gas mark 6.

Tightly wrap the beetroots in foil and put on a baking tray. Bake for 50 minutes, turning them halfway through. Pierce one with a knife; there should be no resistance.

Meanwhile, make the curds: gently heat the milk, lemon juice and salt to 40°C (105°F) on a thermometer, or until it feels as if it is at blood temperature. If it gets too hot, it won't work.

Take off the heat and gently stir in the rennet in one direction. Allow to rest for 30 minutes; it will look a bit scrambled, as if it is separating, which of course it is.

Lay a muslin cloth or clean tea towel in a sieve set over a bowl and carefully pour the curds into the cloth. Let them sit for 20 minutes. Transfer the curds to a container and reserve the whey for another recipe (see page 185).

Leave the beetroot until cool enough to handle, then peel it and slice into wedges (you may wish to wear plastic gloves for this, as it stains).

To serve, put the beetroot in a bowl, season, then add spoonfuls of curds and a sprinkling of toasted sunflower seeds.

Leek and Cheddar Welsh rarebit

A simple but logical twist on a traditional rarebit. Brown sauce is not essential, but does make a nice addition (for home-made, see page 102).

You can make extra cheese sauce for another day; it's great added to cooked and sliced jacket potatoes and heated in the oven.

SERVES 4

50g unsalted butter
200g (about 3 medium) leeks, roughly chopped and well washed

50g plain flour
200ml whole milk
120g mature Cheddar, grated
2 egg yolks
sea salt and freshly ground black pepper
4 slices of thick wholemeal bread

Put the butter in a saucepan set over a low heat, melt, then add the leeks and gently sweat until very soft. Add the flour and stir, cooking for 1 minute. Now gradually add the milk and bring to a simmer for 1 minute. Allow to cool a little, then fold in the cheese, then the yolks, and season.

Meanwhile, grill the bread on one side, turn over and spread generously with the cheese sauce. Place back under the grill and cook until the cheese is golden and bubbling.

Serve with brown sauce.

Summer quiche

When mixing up the milk and eggs for the custard here, we add tomato purée and whisk it in; this gives a tomato flavour running all the way through. Different, impressive and easy.

You can add lots of different vegetables to a quiche. Some things you can get away with uncooked: peas and tomatoes, for example, can be thrown straight in as they will cook in the heat of the egg mix. Others will have to be cooked first, such as broccoli, which is quite hard so would need blanching for a few minutes first in boiling water. We use cream cheese in this recipe, but feel free to change that to ricotta or cottage cheese, according to your mood or what you have in the fridge. The recipe asks for a 23cm diameter, 2.5cm deep fluted flan ring with a removable base; if you don't have one, use the nearest thing, then treat yourself to one some time.

There are so many variations to a quiche; the permutations are endless and entirely up to you. However, try adding a pinch of mustard or some dried herbs to the pastry. Or how about substituting the whipping cream with sour cream?

SERVES 8

175g plain flour, plus more to dust
100g unsalted butter, chopped
1 egg yolk, plus 4 whole eggs
sea salt and freshly ground black pepper
200ml whole milk
200ml whipping cream
70g tomato purée
sunflower oil, for the flan ring
80g frozen peas, defrosted
80g frozen broad beans, defrosted, or you can use fresh if you wish (this is the storecupboard version)

80g cherry tomatoes, halved
125g soft cream cheese

Put the flour in a blender or food processor with the butter, egg yolk and seasoning, then pulse until the mix comes together and forms a dough. Or you can rub the butter in with your fingers and then mix in the egg yolk. Let the pastry rest for 10 minutes

Meanwhile, prepare the filling. In a bowl, whisk the 4 eggs well, then mix in the milk, cream and tomato purée and season well.

Preheat the oven to 180°C/fan 160°C/gas mark 4.

Next, lightly flour a worktop and roll out the pastry so it is a little larger than the flan ring, to allow for the sides of the quiche. Brush a 23cm diameter, 2.5cm deep fluted flan ring with oil. To make life easier, place the rolling pin at the edge of the rolled-out sheet closest to you. Carefully lift the edge over the pin, then very gently roll the pin so the pastry rolls itself around the pin, being careful not to press it down. Place it over the flan ring, then do the reverse roll so the pastry gently falls into place. If you already know that, just ignore the last bit. Make sure the pastry fits snugly into the corners.

Using a pair of scissors, trim off the excess but make sure you leave it a little proud, maybe 5mm, to allow for shrinkage. Line the case with greaseproof paper, fill with baking beans if you have them, if not add handfuls of lentils, then bake for 15 minutes. Remove the beans and paper and bake for another 4 or 5 minutes to crisp up.

Allow the case to cool, then scatter the peas, beans and halved tomatoes evenly around the base. Now, be near your stove when you add the rest of the filling: there's little worse than having to walk across the kitchen balancing a dribbling quiche. Now add the milk and egg mix and finish by adding blobs of the cream cheese; just scatter them on top – some will sink and some will stay on top which will give a nice rustic look.

Slide the quiche on to the middle shelf of the oven and bake for 25 minutes until the filling is softly set.

When cooked, remove from the oven. You may be tempted to have a slice, but let it rest for 5 minutes, as it is very difficult to cut when hot. Serve warm or cold.

Portobello mushrooms, red wine and roast garlic lentils

The best part of this dish has to be the lentils; adding the red wine during the cooking process lifts them from a hippy staple to something a bit special. Puy lentils are the little dark green ones; they are from France and grow in a region which is known for its volcanic mounds. There are similar lentils and you will be OK with those if you cannot find Puy.

It's always good to roast more garlic than you need, as you can use it for so many other dishes. Peel it and squeeze out the soft cloves, then mash them with the back of a fork and mix into some mayonnaise. Or try mixing the mashed garlic cloves with some olive oil and a touch of white wine vinegar and drizzle the pungent dressing over a salad of robust leaves.

_____

SERVES 4

2 bulbs of garlic (add a couple more if you want to use roast garlic in other recipes)

olive oil
4 large Portobello mushrooms, wiped clean

sea salt and freshly ground black pepper
250g Puy lentils
150ml red wine, something quite heavy
2 heads of spring greens, finely shredded

Preheat the oven to 180°C/fan 160°C/ gas mark 4. Cut the tops from the bulbs of garlic so that a little of the cloves is exposed, then place each in a small square of foil, big enough to wrap around the bulb. Drizzle in a little olive oil; don't go crazy, ½ tsp is about enough. Wrap each bulb separately in foil so they look like little tight parcels. Place on a large roasting tray, leaving space for the mushrooms later, then put into the hot oven. Let them cook while you do the next step.

Remove the stalks from the mushrooms and discard. Drizzle a little olive oil in the newly made space and season with salt and pepper.

When the garlic has been in the oven for 15 minutes, add the mushrooms to the roasting tray in the spaces you left earlier. Keep them all gill (underside) uppermost, so all the juices stay in the bowl of the mushroom and don't spill out on to the tray.

The mushrooms will take 15 minutes, 20 if they are especially large. By this time your garlic will be cooked also.

Take a large saucepan and add the lentils. Add just enough water to cover and place over a medium heat; you want to cook them gently so they don't break up. As the lentils cook, they will soak up the water. After they have been simmering for 10 minutes, add the wine and finish cooking for

another 5 to 10 minutes. Taste them to make sure they are cooked – if not, leave for another few minutes, but they won't be far off. When the lentils are cooked, turn off the heat and set aside in their cooking liquid to allow the red wine more time to soak in. Remove the mushrooms and garlic from the oven; they will stay warm while you finish the dish.

Now get on with the last stage. Unwrap the foil from the garlic, peel back the papery skins and, using a teaspoon, pop the soft cloves into a little bowl for a minute.

Put a little olive oil in a saucepan, turn on the heat to high and wait until the oil is very hot, then add the greens. Season with salt and pepper, then stir-fry for a few minutes or until wilted but still with a little crispness.

Finally, to serve, drain the liquid from the lentils, then return them to their cooking pan, add salt and pepper, the roasted garlic and a dash of olive oil, and stir. Place a mound of lentils on each of four warmed plates, then add a helping of greens.

Next place a mushroom on top of the greens – but try to keep any juices in place – and serve.

Baked beetroot and apple, celeriac mash and toasted hazelnut oil

This dish marries some really great flavour combinations: the sharp, sweet apple with the earthy beetroot; the apple playing with the celery notes of the celeriac; the nuttiness and crunch of the hazelnuts tying it all together. The sugar and sherry vinegar glaze gives a sweet-and-sour effect. Celeriac is related to celery but the flavour is more earthy and less pronounced. It is quite ugly, but tastes much better than it looks! To prepare it, cut into quarters and peel; it will be easier to handle this way than it is when whole. We bake beetroots with the skins on as it is easier to peel them when they are cooked; you can just push the skins off with your fingers (wear gloves if you like, as they stain). This dish would be great with a big bowl of roast potatoes instead of the mash on a winter's day – that way you could have the spuds in the oven at the same time as the beetroot.

———————

SERVES 4

6 golfball-sized beetroots
3 large potatoes
sea salt and freshly ground black pepper
1 large head of celeriac
50g unsalted butter
100g hazelnuts, smashed up a bit
150ml sunflower oil
2 Braeburn apples
40g soft brown sugar
50ml sherry vinegar (or balsamic vinegar if you don't have that)

Preheat the oven to 200°C/fan 180°C/ gas mark 6. Tightly wrap the beetroots in foil and put them on a baking tray. Bake for 50 minutes, turning halfway. Check they are cooked by piercing with a knife; there should be no resistance.

Meanwhile, prepare the rest of the dish. Peel the potatoes and chop into about 3cm chunks, but don't be too fussy.

Choose a large pan; you are going to add the celeriac to this pan but it cooks quicker than the potatoes, so they need a head start. Fill it with water and add a sprinkle of salt. Add the potatoes to the pan, bring to the boil, then reduce the heat and simmer for 5 minutes

Peel the celeriac and chop into chunks about the same size as the potatoes. Add them to the pan with the potatoes and top up the water if necessary. The flavour of the celeriac will permeate the potatoes.

After about 10 minutes, check the vegetables to make sure they are cooked; they should be soft but not mushy. Drain and mash.

Add the butter, season and put back over a low heat to help evaporate the moisture, as celeriac can get quite waterlogged in the pan. Keep an eye on it; it won't burn if you stir it occasionally. This is good to remember when you have potatoes which are quite mushy; 5 to 10 minutes over a low heat is usually enough to evaporate the water. Set the mash aside to reheat in the same way later.

Put the hazelnuts in a dry frying pan and cook them until they are golden, being careful as they may catch. As soon as they are browned, add the sunflower oil, remove from the heat and allow to cool and infuse. Remove and decant into a small bowl. Don't wash up the frying pan just yet – save yourself a job.

When the beetroots are cooked, remove the foil and leave until cool enough to handle, then slice off the tops and bottoms, peel and cut each into four wedges.

Without peeling, cut the apples into halves, core them, then cut each half into four. Keep to one side.

Wipe out the hazelnut frying pan with kitchen paper. Add the sugar, set over a low heat and let it gently melt. As it starts to melt, add the vinegar; be careful, don't let the sugar burn. Also try not to inhale the pungent steam; the vinegar fumes will burn your nostrils.

Now add the apples and move the slices around the pan to cook and glaze them at the same time. As they start to soften, add the beetroots to glaze also, and season. They should end up a bit sticky. If they don't, cook for a little longer so the juices evaporate.

To serve, reheat the celeriac mash and divide between plates. Top with the glazed beetroots and apples and sprinkle over the hazelnut oil.

Smoky cauliflower, deep-fried kale and caraway

The smokiness of the cauliflower comes from the slight charring to which it is subjected and this gives a new flavour angle to the vegetable. The little jewel in this dish is the deep-fried kale – it tastes completely different to kale that has been cooked in any other way. You can keep some in an airtight container and use it to sprinkle on a salad, and it is even good as a little snack. To save time we are using butter beans from a can, as I'm sure you have enough to do without worrying about cooking those from dried, too. The addition of the caraway seeds helps to sweeten the big flavours in the dish. A nice addition would be a simple tomato salad.

If you have caraway seeds left they can make a nice, unusual addition to Fruity carrot coleslaw (see page 78).

SERVES 4

about 750ml sunflower oil, to deep-fry, plus a little more for the butter beans

200g kale, coarse ribs removed, torn into manageable pieces

sea salt and freshly ground black pepper
20g caraway seeds
1 cauliflower
2 x 400g cans of butter beans, drained and rinsed

Heat a chip pan or a saucepan of sunflower oil – 750ml should be good – until slight smoke rises from it. To test, drop a piece of kale into the oil to see if it crisps up; if not, heat for a little longer. Have a tray ready, lined with kitchen paper.

Using a slotted spoon, carefully add small amounts of kale to the oil; it will crisp up quickly, in around 15 seconds (be careful, it can spit). Use the slotted spoon to remove the kale and drain on the kitchen paper, then season with a little salt. Repeat to cook all the kale.

Next, take a dry frying pan, heat to medium and add the caraway seeds. Stir them around for 30 seconds, then transfer to a little bowl.

Now the cauliflower: remove the green leaves until you are left with just the white cauliflower. Either cut or break into florets; breaking gives a more natural effect. Anyway, wash and drain well. Then put on kitchen paper to dry fully; it won't char if you don't.

Using the same frying pan as for the caraway, heat with no oil until very hot. Add a few pieces of cauliflower to the pan, but do not pile them up, just put in enough to cover the base. They will char quickly, between 5 and 10 seconds. Season them as they char. Check them and, once they have charred, turn them over so that the other side can also be charred.

Meanwhile, in another frying pan, heat a little oil until it is fairly hot, add the butter beans and fry until heated through.

To serve, arrange the butter beans on plates, top with the cauliflower and sprinkle on the kale and caraway seeds.

Roasted acorn squash, truffle oil and peanuts

Acorn squash is so called because of its shape. If you are having trouble getting hold of it, just use butternut squash – they have slightly different flavours but you should spend your time cooking, not shopping. Peanuts are one of those little ingredients you forget about; choose unsalted and try to roast a few extra, as you will definitely eat some before they get to the table. Or keep the extra in the cupboard – they are great for adding to a stir-fry, salad or curry. There are two ways to prepare the squash, so read the recipe first so you know which one you will be doing. And keep the seeds.

You could also try mashing and adding different flavours; squash lend themselves to so many flavours – try chilli, rosemary, nutmeg, garlic...

SERVES 4

1 large acorn squash, or a butternut
if needs must

sunflower oil
sea salt
pinch of ground cinnamon
2 tbsp demerara sugar
80g unsalted peanuts
sprinkle of truffle oil
1 spring onion, finely sliced

Preheat the oven to 200°C/fan 180°C/ gas mark 6.

First of all the squash – you will need a strong knife. You can do this two ways and both ways have their benefits. Number one is to cook it with the skin on, which is easier but means you have to fiddle with it at the end and run the risk of breaking it up. Number two, you can peel the squash first, which is trickier as it is a tough beast, but this way means that at the end you can just easily serve as it is. Some people eat the roasted skin but this can be hit and miss depending on the thickness of the skin.

Lay the squash on its side and cut it in half lengthways. Next cut each half into three, lengthways again. Using a spoon, scoop out the seeds and reserve – you can use them for something else (see right). Now either peel off the skins with a sharp knife or just carry on.

Now, place the wedges in a roasting tray with the flesh side uppermost. Drizzle with a little oil, a sprinkle of salt, the cinnamon and demerara sugar; the sugar will help create colour and stickiness. Bake for 30 minutes or until tender when prodded with a knife.

Place the peanuts on a baking tray and pop in the oven to roast at the same time as you put in the squash. The nuts will only take around 10 minutes to take on some colour, but keep a check on them and turn them once, as they are one of those things that tend to

scorch very rapidly when you are not looking. When the peanuts are golden, remove from the oven and allow to cool. These will store in an airtight container for a couple of weeks.

As soon as the squash is cooked, you are ready to serve. If you have left the skin on, you will need to carefully remove it now.

Place the squash on plates. Drizzle on some truffle oil, being careful, as it is strong. Then add the peanuts and scatter on the spring onion, to give a little bite to the dish. Finally add a sprinkle of sea salt and away you go.

WHAT ABOUT THE SEEDS?

Clean them of the fibrous bits of string and flesh under running water. Pat dry on kitchen paper, then place in a bowl, coat in a drizzle of olive oil and roast on a baking tray for 15 minutes, turning once or twice with a spatula, or until golden. Sprinkle with sea salt and serve, or even try some icing sugar instead of salt. A snack using your leftovers – very nice.

Jerusalem artichoke, white wine and thyme pie

Just to clear up any confusion, globe artichokes are the big green spiky things and Jerusalem artichokes are the little knobbly things that look like potatoes. They have an unusual sweet flavour that is difficult to describe. Word of warning: they oxidise quickly, so you need to peel them and drop them into cold water mixed with the juice of half a lemon to prevent discoloration. Taking a few nice ingredients such as white wine and artichokes and dropping them into something as humble as a pie seems a little rebellious, but let's do it anyway.

Try swapping the white wine for red wine and the thyme for rosemary, simple substitutions that give totally different results.

SERVES 4

juice of ½ lemon
1.4kg Jerusalem artichokes
(it may seem like a lot but you
will lose some when peeling)

splash of sunflower oil
1 large onion, finely chopped
2 garlic cloves, finely chopped
1 large potato, peeled
and grated

400ml white wine, something
quite dry, plus more if needed

small sprig of thyme
400g shop-bought puff pastry
plain flour, to dust
1 tsp cornflour (try to make
sure it is a level teaspoon, this
stuff thickens aggressively)

sea salt and freshly ground
black pepper

whole milk, to brush

Have a bowl of water to hand with the lemon juice squeezed into it. Peel the artichokes; they are tricky, so be prepared for some fun. As you peel them, drop them straight into the water to prevent discoloration.

In a large saucepan, pour a touch of sunflower oil and place over a medium heat. Next add the onion, garlic and potato and fry until golden. The mixture may stick, especially the potato, so give it all a good scrape. This will give colour to the overall dish.

Next, tip all the fried vegetables into a bowl and set aside. Add a little more oil to the pan to heat, then drain the artichokes and add to the hot oil, stirring over a high heat until golden on all sides.

Add the reserved vegetables, wine and sprig of thyme (this will infuse the vegetables with its flavour; you will lift it out later). Top up with cold water to cover and simmer very gently for 10–15 minutes or until the artichokes are tender when pierced with a knife.

Preheat the oven to 180°C/fan 160°C/gas mark 4. Fish out the sprig of thyme and throw it away. Then, using a slotted spoon, remove all the vegetables, draining well. Share them between four individual pie dishes or your favourite bowls – ovenproof of course – or just spoon into one large pie dish.

Now, increase the heat under the remaining liquid (that's why you removed the vegetables, or they would have fallen to pieces). Bubble the liquid to evaporate by half, to concentrate the colour and flavours.

Meanwhile, roll out the pastry on a lightly floured worktop and cut out the pastry lids, making them slightly bigger than the pie dishes or dish to allow for shrinkage.

When the liquor has evaporated by half, reduce the heat, mix the cornflour with a little cold water so it is the consistency of single cream and carefully whisk the cornflour into the liquid. It will thicken quickly. Season and add a little more wine if it is too thick for your taste.

Pour a little of the sauce on to the vegetables, brush a little milk around the rim of the dish, place the pastry on top and press to seal the edges. Brush more milk on top of the pastry, then pierce a vent hole in the top. You can make shapes with pastry scraps to decorate the pies if you are feeling adventurous. If you are not, just put them in the oven and bake small pies for 10 minutes or a large pie for 35–45 minutes, or until the pastry is risen and golden.

Serve immediately.

Baked Stilton pudding with pickled grapes

This is a hearty dish, perfect to serve to those who think they will still be hungry after a vegetarian meal. You will need to leave it to rest for around 15 minutes after removing from the oven, or it will be difficult to cut. We pair grapes with this dish as they work well with blue cheese and, when pickled, help to balance the richness of the pudding. It's good to pickle extra grapes to add to a salad or even a sandwich with a good strong cheese.

You can make this pudding a little more fancy by cooking in individual moulds and serving topped with the grapes; this way they are good for a dinner party (but will need less time in the oven, so keep an eye on them).

SERVES 4–6

For the pickled grapes
    small bunch of red grapes
    300ml red wine
    50ml balsamic vinegar
    80g soft brown sugar
    10 black peppercorns

For the pudding
    3 eggs
    400g whipping cream
    180g fine white breadcrumbs
    375g Stilton, crumbled
    sea salt and freshly ground
    black pepper

Preheat the oven to 170°C/fan 150°C/ gas mark 3½.

Start with the grapes: wash and pick small branches of them from the stems and place on a baking sheet lined with greaseproof paper; leaving them on a branch creates an interesting garnish. Leave at the bottom of the oven, where it is coolest, for 45 minutes; this will semi-dry them and enable them to absorb the pickling liquor.

Meanwhile, make the pickling liquor: put the wine, vinegar, sugar and peppercorns into a saucepan and bring to the boil. Transfer the liquid to a bowl and leave until cold. Remove the grapes from the oven and add to the pickling liquor while they are warm. Cool, then refrigerate.

Now for the pudding. Preheat the oven once more to 170°C/fan 150°C/gas mark 3½.

Beat the eggs, add the cream and breadcrumbs and mix. Fold in the cheese and season.

Line a 20 x 10 x 8cm loaf tin with greaseproof paper, pour in the batter and bake for 45 minutes. This may seem like a short cooking time, but in theory you are only actually cooking the eggs.

When the pudding is cooked, remove it from the oven and allow to cool for around 15 minutes. Then place a tray or large plate on top and turn out. Peel off the greaseproof paper and serve in thick slices with piles of drained pickled grapes.

(If you are making this ahead of time, allow the pudding to become completely cold on a wire rack, then cover and refrigerate. The next day, carve thick slices of it, lay on a buttered baking tray, cover lightly with foil and place in an oven preheated to 200°C/fan 180°C/gas mark 6. Cook for 10 minutes, or until piping hot.)

Cheddar and chutney bread and butter pudding with greens

Indulgent, satisfying and relatively easy to make. Along with being cost effective, this is a good all-rounder. Firstly the Red onion chutney (see page 106) keeps well, so it should always be around. Next, you can use any bread you wish, even some of those dry crusts which you keep dodging. Finally you probably have some eggs and milk in the fridge, so all in all this is going to be easy. The greens balance the dish, but use any greens or even mix a couple of different cabbages.

There are lots of variations you can try for this recipe: blue Stilton and spinach, English Brie and tomato, red Leicester and sage… That should keep you going for now.

SERVES 4

5 medium or large eggs (it won't make a great deal of difference)

500ml whole or semi-skimmed milk (you choose)

sea salt and freshly ground black pepper

softened unsalted butter, to spread
5 slices of bread (your choice)
125g Red onion chutney (see page 106)

150g good strong Cheddar, grated
splash of sunflower oil
1 large head of Savoy cabbage, quartered, cored and shredded

Preheat the oven to 180°C/fan 160°C/gas mark 4.

Break the eggs into a large mixing bowl. No shell, please. Beat briskly with a whisk, then add the milk, season and whisk again.

Butter the bread, but don't be fussy. Cut the slices into quarters, then line an ovenproof dish with some of the bread. Sprinkle evenly with some chutney and cheese. Repeat until you have used up all the ingredients, but hold back a sprinkling of cheese; you will see why in a bit.

Now move your dish closer to the oven; that way you don't have to walk too far with a dish full of liquid. Pour the milk mix on to the bread, give the bread a bit of a press down so it absorbs the milk, then add the last sprinkling of cheese – this will help with the overall appearance of the pudding.

Bake the pudding for 40 minutes or until golden and risen.

Remove from the oven and let it settle. It may appear to be uncooked because it will be wobbly, but give it 10 minutes to rest and it will settle down.

While you wait, put a little oil in a large saucepan, heat it and then add the shredded cabbage. Season with salt and pepper and fry over a medium heat for 3 minutes. Cover, reduce the heat and let the cabbage steam.

Stir once or twice and, after about 8 minutes, check it to make sure it is not catching on the pan and to see if it is cooked to your preference; if not, give it a few more minutes. Frying your cabbage this way gives a nutty flavour to the end result.

This should give time for the pudding to calm down – if it's too hot it is difficult to serve and rather sloppy. Place a couple of spoons of greens on to a plate and spread them around to make a base. Now take a spoonful of the bread and butter pudding, place it on top of the greens and serve.

Mature Cheddar and Savoy cabbage pudding with ale

This originated from an Italian recipe which used fontina and chicken stock; we have created this British and vegetarian version, but I'm sure the Italians would still love it. If you don't have any stale bread, just leave some slices hanging around the kitchen for a few hours before you start cooking, or when you leave for work in the morning. The drier the bread the better, as it soaks up the juices. We used to make a version of this at our original York restaurant and people would call before arriving to make sure it was still on the menu.

SERVES 4

For the pudding
sea salt and freshly ground
black pepper

1 small Savoy cabbage
120g unsalted butter
4 thick slices of white bread,
preferably a couple of days old,
broken into pieces

250g mature Cheddar, grated

For the ale reduction
350ml ale (a dark ale such as
Black Sheep is best)

75g granulated sugar

Fill a large saucepan with cold water and 2 tbsp of salt and bring to the boil. Have a large bowl of cold water ready.

Remove any bruised or rough-looking outer leaves from the cabbage. Cut the cabbage in half, making sure you go through the core, then cut into quarters. Remove the core and separate the leaves. Wash well, as Savoy has lots of hiding places for soil and dirt.

Plunge the cabbage leaves into the boiling water in small batches and cook for 5 or 6 minutes, or until tender. Using a slotted spoon, remove the cabbage from the water (reserve the cooking water) and add to a bowl of cold water to prevent overcooking; this will also help to keep the colour. Drain.

Pour 100ml of the hot cabbage cooking water into a large mixing bowl (pour away the rest), add the butter and allow to melt. Add the bread to the bowl and mix to allow the liquid to absorb.

Take four 150ml microwaveable pudding dishes and line each with one large dark green cabbage leaf and one lighter green leaf. This will look nice when it is turned out. Add a few pieces of bread, season with salt and pepper, then add some grated cheese. Press down firmly and repeat the process:

cabbage, bread, seasoning and cheese. Don't forget to press down. Cover and refrigerate until needed.

Simmer the ale with the sugar until it has reduced to about half its original volume. Season with salt.

To serve, place a lid loosely on a pudding basin and microwave on medium (800W) for 1 minute, then remove and carefully turn upside down, being careful of your hands, to allow all the liquids to circulate. Turn the right way up again and heat for a further 1½ minutes or until piping hot. Repeat to cook all four puddings. (If you haven't got a microwave, place the basins in a steamer and cook for 15 minutes.)

Remove the lids and carefully invert on to plates. Add a little of the ale reduction and serve simply with a few boiled potatoes, or turn it into something more substantial with some roasted root vegetables.

Double-baked goat's Cheddar puddings, baked tomatoes and Little Gem

Goat's Cheddar is a wonderful thing; there are lots of varieties on the market and if you can get hold of a mature version it will make this recipe even better. These puddings are based on soufflés but are denser, so make for a more substantial dish. As they need to be baked twice, you could actually cook them the day before. It is important to cool the puddings before the second bake, to create a lovely crust.

You can try adding different cheeses to the pudding, such as regular Cheddar or Stilton. You can also vary the dish by adding baked mushrooms (see page 153). One meal can actually become several variations, with a bit of imagination.

SERVES 6

40g unsalted butter, plus more
for the ramekins

40g plain flour, plus more for
the ramekins

225ml warm whole milk
150ml whipping cream
4 eggs, separated
sea salt and freshly ground
black pepper

175g goat's Cheddar, grated
4 large ripe tomatoes
a little sunflower oil
2 heads of Little Gem lettuce
1 quantity Fried onion vinaigrette
(see page 108)

Preheat the oven to 150°C/fan 130°C/ gas mark 2.

Melt the butter in a saucepan, tip in the flour and cook gently for around 2 minutes.

Gradually whisk in the warm milk and heat until the sauce starts to bubble, then finally add the cream.

Cool a little, then whisk in the egg yolks. (If you add them while the sauce is still hot, the yolks will turn into scrambled eggs.)

Next whisk the whites in a clean bowl – I'm not suggesting you have bad habits, it's just that egg whites will not rise in a greasy bowl – with a pinch of salt until soft peaks form.

Using a spatula, fold the whites into the sauce, then season the mix with salt and pepper and finally add the cheese. Be careful at this stage, you don't want to undo all that whipping by being too heavy with your folding.

Now take six ramekins – or those silicone pudding moulds are really good – butter and flour them, then line with circles of baking parchment. Add the mix to them, making sure you get some of the cheese which will have fallen to the base of the saucepan. If you have any mixture left, bake it in another buttered and floured container; it can be your tester.

Bake in the oven for 1 hour; they will be slightly risen but still a little wobbly. Allow them to cool in the moulds.

Wait until the puddings are cold, then remove from the moulds and refrigerate. You can reheat them later, or even the next day.

When you are ready to serve the meal, preheat the oven to 160°C/fan 140°C/gas mark 3. Cut the tomatoes in half or quarters, brush with a little oil and season with salt and pepper. Pop them in a baking tray, place at the bottom of the oven and cook for 20 minutes. At the same time, place the puddings on a baking tray lined with baking parchment on the top shelf of the oven, also for 20 minutes.

Meanwhile, halve the lettuces, brush with oil and season. Place on a third baking tray. When the puddings and tomatoes have been in the oven for 15 minutes, add the lettuces for the last 5 minutes.

To serve, check the puddings are hot, put them on warmed plates and serve with the tomatoes and lettuces. Drizzle the tomatoes and lettuces with the Fried onion vinaigrette, or serve the vinaigrette underneath the puddings.

SIDE DISHES

Raspberry, pickled rhubarb and pink peppercorn salad

Summery, zingy and a bit quirky. This fruity salad would work nicely with the richness of the Cauliflower sheep's cheese with fried mustard crumbs (see page 68). This is the type of dish that benefits from a few hours of infusing. Pink peppercorns are actually not a true pepper but rather a dried berry from a shrub. If you have trouble finding them, just give a grind of black pepper and tell everybody yours are the extra-ripened kind. The pickled rhubarb will keep for a week in your fridge. You can keep the pickling liquor and use it to pickle something else, cucumbers for example.

Next time, try using strawberries instead of raspberries.

SERVES 4

100ml white wine vinegar
80g granulated sugar
1cm piece of root ginger, sliced
1 tsp sea salt
6 black peppercorns
250g rhubarb
1 tsp pink peppercorns
100g raspberries
extra virgin olive oil

First, make the pickling liquor. Pour 50ml of water into a saucepan and add the vinegar, sugar, ginger, salt and black peppercorns. Bring to the boil, then turn the heat off and allow to cool a little before transferring to a separate bowl and allowing to cool completely.

Discard any leaves from the rhubarb, wash the sticks, then slice across into 1cm pieces.

When the pickling liquor has cooled, strain to remove the bits and pieces. Add the rhubarb and pink peppercorns. Ideally leave this for a few hours to help it to pickle but, if you don't have the luxury of time, make it 30 minutes.

To serve, use a slotted spoon to remove the rhubarb and a few peppercorns to a serving dish, sprinkle on the raspberries and gently fold them into the rhubarb, then finally add a glug of olive oil.

Kohlrabi, gherkin and apple salad

If you have not used kohlrabi before, give it a go. Its flavour hovers between cabbage, radish and broccoli and it looks like… errrrm… kohlrabi. It is technically an autumn vegetable but you can get hold of it earlier – it's just a bit smaller. It can be eaten cooked or raw; we have gone for raw in this recipe to create a crunchy salad. Try serving it with a Scotch duck egg (see page 95); the crunchiness will go well with the soft egg.

For a quick variation, try using different apples, such as Cox's or Granny Smith, but keep them on the tarter side. You could also change the cider vinegar to white wine vinegar instead – go ahead and experiment.

SERVES 4

80ml sunflower oil
2 tbsp cider vinegar
50g brown sugar
sea salt and freshly ground
black pepper

1 kohlrabi, the size of a tennis ball
(funny, some are a similar colour, too)

small jar of gherkins
2 Braeburn apples
small amount of chives – we are
talking 6 stems

First make the simple dressing, to allow time for the sugar to dissolve, which in turn will balance the acidity. Simply put the oil, vinegar and sugar in a plastic bowl, season with salt and black pepper, mix and set aside. Stir occasionally and, by the time you have prepared everything else, it should be done.

Now the kohlrabi. Take a small slice from the top and bottom. With a sharp knife or decent peeler, remove the skin, as you would for a turnip. The next step is to take thin (about 5mm) slices of the kohlrabi, lay them flat, then slice into sticks.

Stir the sticks of kohlrabi into the dressing. Then slice 10 of the gherkins, each one into three is enough. Pop into the bowl.

Cut the apples into quarters, but do not peel, as the skin gives a good colour. With a sharp knife, slice out the core. Lay the quarters on a chopping board and slice into thin wedges; immediately add them to the bowl and gently mix so they don't discolour.

Finally, using a pair of sharp scissors (always good to have around, especially for herbs), finely snip the chives into the bowl and gently mix.

Your salad is now ready to serve. It will not keep for long, as the apples will soften and discolour eventually, so try to use it as soon as possible for the optimum crunch.

Whey-poached purple-sprouting broccoli with sesame

You will need the whey from the Baked beetroot, home-made curds and toasted sunflower seeds recipe (see page 148) for this dish; no point going through the process of making it again. Poaching the broccoli in whey gives an unusual tang, and it's also a good way to use a byproduct. If you are having problems getting hold of purple-sprouting broccoli because it's out of season, just use regular broccoli and wait until next year when it's available again. Now there's something to look forward to.

Toasted nuts also go well with broccoli; try almonds or even cashews.

SERVES 4

400g purple-sprouting broccoli,
no yellow leaves or limp stems

1 quantity whey (see page 148)
3 tsp sesame seeds
sea salt and freshly ground
black pepper

unsalted butter or olive oil

First let us prepare the broccoli: you need to keep most of the stem, so just slice off the first 2cm, which should be enough to remove the woody bit. Pull off some of the coarser leaves, but leave the others as they are tasty and look good.

Next pour the whey into a saucepan and bring it to a simmer.

As you wait, take a dry frying pan and heat to medium. Throw in the sesame seeds and quickly fry until golden – this will take about 30 seconds. Tip them into a container so they don't burn.

Boil half a kettle of water. When the whey comes to a simmer, add the broccoli, pouring in some of the hot water from the kettle so the broccoli is just covered, if needed. Simmer for 3 minutes, then remove with a slotted spoon and place in a serving dish.

Sprinkle the broccoli with the sesame seeds, salt and pepper, finishing with either knobs of butter or a dash of olive oil.

Little Marmite potatoes

Originally a byproduct of the brewing industry, Marmite is great for vegetarian cooking. If you ever have a gravy or soup which is lacking that certain something, just add 1 tsp of Marmite and taste the difference – it will give depth. In this recipe we have paired it with the neutral flavour of potatoes, which works very well. Get ready for the aromas coming from your kitchen with this one.

For something a little different, allow the potatoes to cool and serve as a salad, dressed with a little olive oil and some chopped spring onions.

SERVES 4

2 tsp sea salt
500g little potatoes (the ready-washed bags are great)

60g Marmite

Bring a large pan of water to the boil and add the salt and potatoes. When they are cooked, in 15–20 minutes, drain off the water. Meanwhile, preheat the oven to 200°C/ fan 180°C/gas mark 6.

Warm 2 tbsp of water in a plastic bowl in a microwave – or take it from a recently boiled kettle – then mix in the Marmite; this will help it to distribute evenly.

Put the potatoes on a roasting tray and dress evenly with the Marmite, giving a good mix to coat the potatoes while being careful not to break them up.

Pop into the oven and roast for 8–10 minutes, giving a quick turn halfway through. Watch them, as they can easily catch and burn. The Marmite should bake on to the potatoes and make them sticky.

Serve, but be careful, as the Marmite can make the potatoes very hot.

Radishes with garlic milk dressing

Radishes are amazing little things. We used to slice them and add them to salads but we decided one day to make a feature of them. We have tried quite a few dressings, but this version is the most popular. Cooking the garlic in milk tones it down and the flavour infuses the milk in the dressing. Keeping the radish leaves attached makes this a pretty salad and you can eat them, too.

Radishes lend themselves to a few other interesting ingredients: instead of garlic milk try toasted sesame seeds or infused hazelnut oil (see page 157).

SERVES 4

6 garlic cloves, peeled and roughly chopped

200ml whole milk
large bunch of pink radishes
sea salt and freshly ground
black pepper

Place the garlic in a small saucepan with the milk and bring to a very gentle simmer until the garlic is very soft, which should take 5–8 minutes. Allow to cool completely.

Wash the radishes but leave the leaves attached. Make sure they are bright coloured and perky and throw away any that aren't. Pat the radishes and leaves dry with kitchen paper.

With a hand-held blender, blend the garlic and milk until smooth, then season.

Arrange the radishes on a plate, keeping the globe ends together so you can dress them all at once.

Drizzle the garlic milk over the globes, leaving the leaves free and clean.

To eat, pick up by the leaves and eat the radish, dipping it in the garlic milk. Don't forget to eat the leaves – their flavour will surprise you.

Brown butter parsnip mash

This is one of those dishes which you just want to eat on its own. A simple thing such as browning the butter seems to transform the dish. Remember to dry the parsnips in the pan on a low heat; this removes the excess water and therefore concentrates the flavour. You can try the same method if you are making mashed potatoes and the potatoes have become a bit waterlogged.

If by some strange chance you have some of the mash left, let it go cold and, the next day, shape into little cakes. Shallow-fry them and serve with a fried egg.

SERVES 4

1kg parsnips, peeled and trimmed of their tops

80g unsalted butter
sea salt and freshly ground black pepper
pinch of nutmeg

Slice the prepared parsnips into a saucepan, cover with water, bring to the boil, then simmer until soft when pierced with a knife.

Meanwhile, put the butter in a small frying pan over a medium heat. Hold at this temperature until you see the butter start to appear golden. It's the milk solids which are actually browning and giving the colour and flavour. Once this has happened, remove from the heat and transfer to a little bowl to prevent it over-cooking.

When the parsnips are cooked, drain well, return them to the pan and put it over a low heat. Stir to prevent sticking and continue for around 4 minutes. You will see the steam drifting from the pan – that's the water leaving.

Next mash the parsnips, season and add the nutmeg and brown butter. Mix well and serve.

Honey-glazed carrots with chervil

A nice way to cook carrots, which accentuates their sweetness. Chervil is a pretty herb and always makes a good garnish, but equally works well as an ingredient. It has a mild aniseed flavour. You may find it hard to get hold of, so you could use tarragon instead, or why not try growing chervil – it makes a pretty plant. This would make a good friend for the Jerusalem artichoke, white wine and thyme pie (see page 165).

For some fun variations try different types of honey; you could experiment until you find your favourite.

SERVES 4

500g carrots of your choice, such as Chantenay or heritage

sea salt
2 tbsp runny honey, again your choice

small bunch of chervil

Preheat the oven to 180°C/fan160°C/gas mark 4.

You need to slightly cook the carrots first, because completely cooking them in the oven can make them tough. Bring a large pan of water to the boil to which you have added a little salt. While it heats up, peel the carrots and remove the tops.

When the water boils, add the carrots. Simmer for 5 minutes, then remove with a slotted spoon and put straight into a roasting tray.

Drizzle with the honey and season with a little more salt, give a stir so that the carrots are evenly coated, then pop them in the hot oven for 10–15 minutes or until tender when pierced with a knife and sticky.

As the carrots roast, chop the chervil finely. When it comes to the last 5 minutes of roasting, bring the carrots out of the oven, give them a stir and sprinkle on most of the chervil, then pop back in the oven to finish.

Serve immediately, sprinkling the carrots with the remaining chervil.

Roast turnips and caramelised apples with cider glaze

Just to clear a few things up first: when I say turnips I mean the ones that are white with a light purple tinge; the vegetable which is pale yellow with a purple top is a swede. Both are good, but the flavour of swede tends to be a bit stronger. Roasting the turnips brings on a slightly different flavour, more pronounced, while the sweetness of the apples and cider glaze add an almost sweet and sour aspect.

A little tip when choosing turnips: give them a good squeeze. They need to be hard as a rock; any softness means they are likely to be woody inside.

SERVES 4

800g turnips – it seems a lot but you will lose quite a bit in the peeling

sunflower oil
sea salt
2 Granny Smith apples
50g granulated sugar, plus a sprinkling to season

100ml cider, preferably dry
2 tbsp cider vinegar

Preheat the oven to 190°C/fan 170°C/gas mark 5.

Turnips first: slice off the tops and bottoms and cut into quarters so you end up with wedges – they are easier to peel like this than when they are whole. Using a small sharp knife, peel off the skins. Pop the wedges into a roasting tray, drizzle with a little oil and season with salt. Use your hands to mix them up so that they are all coated. Place in the oven; they will take around 30 minutes to cook depending on size. You will know when they are ready as they will be nice and soft when you give them a little prod and they will have some golden colour to them. Give them a turn now and again.

While the turnips cook, prepare the apples. Stand them up and cut them in half, then remove the core and cut each half into five wedges; this will help the dish to look pretty, as you are mimicking the shape of the turnips. Put the apple wedges in a bowl, give them a glug of oil and season with salt and a good sprinkle of sugar.

Into a frying pan (using a frying pan helps the glaze to reduce quicker, due to the surface area) pour the cider, vinegar and 50g of sugar. Bring to the boil, then simmer for 5 minutes. Transfer to a bowl, but don't clean the pan.

Five minutes before the turnips are finished, take the frying pan, give it a quick wipe, then put it over a high heat with no oil. When it is very hot, add the apple wedges and flash-fry on both sides to caramelise them; this will take a few seconds, so be careful, and they may stick. Turn the heat off and leave the apples to finish cooking in the remaining heat.

Meanwhile remove the turnips from the oven, transfer to a serving bowl, add the apple wedges, then drizzle with the cider glaze. Or add the apples to the roasting tray with the turnips, drizzle over the glaze and mix carefully. Serve.

If you like the apple and turnip mix you can create another similar dish by peeling and chopping the turnips, peeling, coring and chopping the apples, then boiling them together. Drain well, then mash with a spot of butter and seasoning.

PUDDINGS

Flourless chocolate and raspberry cakes with rose cream

These cakes are outrageously rich. Buy the best chocolate you can afford, as it will make a huge difference to the flavour. A word of warning: do make sure that your microwave is on the lowest setting and that you stir the chocolate every 10 seconds, as it can burn so easily. For a good presentation, when the cakes are cold, carefully slice off the domed tops and turn each one upside down so that you have a neat little tower. You can even sprinkle rose petals around, if you wish.

MAKES 10

For the cake
- 300g 70% cocoa solids chocolate, chopped
- 125g unsalted butter, chopped, plus more for the moulds
- 6 eggs
- 175g granulated sugar
- 100g raspberries, halved

For the rose cream
- 4 tbsp rose water
- 1 tbsp icing sugar, sifted
- 100ml double cream, cold

To decorate
- 10 raspberries
- icing sugar, to dust
- 10 unsprayed rose petals, washed (optional)

Preheat the oven to 170°C/fan 150°C/gas mark 3½.

Melt 225g of the chocolate – the rest we will use soon – and all the butter in the microwave on a low heat, stirring every 10 seconds. Or melt it in a heatproof bowl set over simmering water (don't let the bowl touch the water). Set aside to cool a little.

Whisk the eggs, gradually adding the sugar until you have a frothy, glossy mix. Add the cooled chocolate and butter, mixing thoroughly, then fold in most of the remaining chocolate (saving 10 pieces) and the raspberries.

Lightly butter 10 muffin moulds and divide the batter evenly between them. Stick one piece of chocolate in the middle of each and bake for 15–20 minutes, or until the cakes have risen and are firm, but still a bit gooey in the middle. Leave to cool in the moulds on a wire rack while you make the cream.

Whip together the rose water, icing sugar and cream to soft peaks. Cover and keep in the fridge until ready to serve.

Decorate each cake with a dollop of rose cream, a raspberry and a dusting of icing sugar. Add a single rose petal, if you want.

Little cherry Bakewell tarts

These individual tarts look great as a display. Because they are small, we roll
the pastry between two pieces of baking parchment to make it easier to handle.
A good tip is to use little 'bean bags' made from lentils or rice wrapped in foil
for the blind-baking; this makes sure the beans fit into the little pastry cases and
are easy to remove afterwards. Serve with Toasted marzipan custard (see page 118);
an absolute must! (It is a logical partner because of the almonds.) Don't forget
you can use any fruit which is in season instead of cherries; try raspberries,
or even just Lemon curd (see page 113).

MAKES 6

60g ground almonds
1 quantity sweet Basic shortcrust
pastry (see page 109)

60g self-raising flour, plus more
to dust

3 eggs, lightly beaten
125g sunflower oil
125g golden caster sugar
½ tsp almond extract
pinch of sea salt
75g ripe cherries, pitted and quartered
6 heaped tbsp cherry jam, preferably
home-made

40g flaked almonds
icing sugar, to dust

Preheat the oven to 160°C/fan 140°C/gas mark 3. Spread the ground almonds on a baking tray and toast for 15–20 minutes, or until golden brown. Keep an eye on them and turn them with a spatula every 5 minutes so they cook evenly and don't scorch. Allow to cool.

Cut baking parchment into 12 x 14cm squares. Divide the pastry into 6 balls and roll each out between 2 of the squares.

Next, remove the top layer of parchment and place the pastry gently into a muffin mould, so the remaining baking parchment is on the bottom. Dip your fingertips into a little flour, then carefully press the pastry into the mould, leaving some overhanging the edge (you can trim it later if you want). Take the little 'bean bags' mentioned in the recipe introduction, place them in the cases and blind-bake for 15 minutes; the pastry edges should have started to brown.

Carefully remove the bean bags, then prick the pastry all over with a fork and return to the oven for a further 12–15 minutes, or until light golden brown. Leave to cool on a cooling rack, keeping them in the muffin tray to maintain the shape.

Meanwhile, whisk the eggs, oil and caster sugar in a large mixing bowl (or use a food mixer fitted with the beater attachment), then add the flour, ground almonds, almond extract and salt. Lastly fold in the cherries.

Making sure your pastry cases are cool, spread 1 heaped tbsp of cherry jam in each, then divide the cake batter evenly between them. Sprinkle the flaked almonds over the tops, then bake for 25–30 minutes, or until firm to the touch and a skewer inserted into the middle comes out clean. If the flaked almonds start to get too brown before the sponge is cooked, cover the tarts loosely with foil hats. Cook until firm.

Allow to cool in the moulds for 10 minutes before carefully transferring to a wire rack. Once completely cool, trim the edges if necessary, or if you are feeling fussy. You can then dust them with icing sugar and serve in the baking parchment, or remove from the parchment and serve on plates with Toasted marzipan custard (see page 118).

Lemon curd treacle tart

Most treacle tart recipes call for just golden syrup, but we use black treacle and dates here, too, which give a rich, sour depth that works beautifully with the fresh acidity of lemons. Of course you can use shop-bought lemon curd, but it's much more satisfying, not to mention more delicious, to make your own (see page 113).

––––––––

SERVES 6–8

1 quantity sweet Basic shortcrust pastry (see page 109)

100g dates, pitted
½ tsp bicarbonate of soda
3 eggs, lightly beaten
2 tbsp (50g) black treacle
4 tbsp (100g) golden syrup
100ml double cream, plus more to serve

150g fresh white breadcrumbs
pinch of sea salt
5 heaped tbsp lemon curd, preferably home-made (see page 113)

icing sugar, to dust

Preheat the oven to 160°C/fan 140°C/ gas mark 3. Roll the pastry out between two sheets of baking parchment (see page 109).

Ease the pastry, still sandwiched between the sheets of baking parchment, into a 20cm, 3.5cm deep sandwich cake tin, pressing it gently into the bottom and leaving some overhanging the edge. Cover the base with baking beans (or any dried beans) and 'blind-bake' for 15 minutes, by which time the pastry edges should have started to brown. Carefully remove the beans along with the top layer of baking parchment, then prick the pastry all over with a fork and return to the oven for 12–15 minutes, or until the pastry is a light golden brown. Leave to cool on a wire rack.

Meanwhile, make the filling. Put the dates in a saucepan with 150ml of water and the bicarbonate of soda and set over a medium heat until the water has mostly reduced and the dates have softened, about 5 minutes. The bicarbonate will turn the dates a dark green colour, but don't be alarmed!

Blitz the contents of the pan, using a hand-held blender or a food processor, then combine with the eggs, treacle, golden syrup, cream, breadcrumbs and salt in a large mixing bowl.

Make sure your pastry case is cool, then spread the lemon curd evenly over it. Now pour the treacle mix on top and bake for 45–50 minutes or until set and firm to touch.

Leave to cool in the tin on a cooling rack, then, with a knife or a pair of scissors, carefully trim the overhanging pastry. Dust with icing sugar and serve with plenty of whipped double cream.

Boozy prune and honey cake

Soaking prunes in brandy (we like to use Somerset cider brandy) makes this a great dinner party dessert, and it can be made the day before. Serve it with good-quality vanilla ice cream or crème fraîche. If you want to add a further touch, soak a few more prunes, say 12, adding another 50ml more brandy to the soaking liquid; reserve them and use as a garnish at the end. Add 2 on top of each portion and drizzle a little glaze around the plate with a scoop of clotted cream. You will be very popular.

SERVES 6–8

150g prunes, pitted
50ml brandy
unsalted butter, for the tin
25g walnuts
3 eggs, lightly beaten
150g sunflower oil
125g light muscovado sugar
4 tbsp honey, plus 2 tbsp more to glaze
150g self-raising flour
½ tsp baking powder
pinch of sea salt
finely grated zest of 1 orange

The night (or at least a couple of hours) before, cover the prunes with the brandy and leave to soak.

When you're ready to make the cake, preheat the oven to 155°C/fan 135°C/gas mark 3. Butter a 26 x 12cm loaf tin and line the base and sides with baking parchment.

Toast the walnuts on a baking tray in the oven for 20–25 minutes, or until golden brown. Allow to cool, then roughly chop.

In a large mixing bowl (or a food mixer fitted with the beater attachment), whisk together the eggs, oil, sugar and the 4 tbsp of honey. Add the flour, baking powder and salt. Drain the prunes (reserving the brandy), then fold them in along with the orange zest and walnuts.

Spoon into the prepared tin and bake for 50–55 minutes or until firm to the touch. A skewer inserted into the middle of the cake should come out clean. Allow to cool in the tin for 10 minutes before turning out on to a wire rack.

Meanwhile, make a glaze: heat the 2 tbsp of honey with 1 tbsp of water in a small pan over a medium heat, then add to the reserved brandy. While the cake is still warm, prick the top with a skewer and brush the glaze all over. (Or reserve a little glaze to drizzle over each portion, see recipe introduction.)

Meringues

A great way to use up leftover egg whites, meringue is easy to make and is a lovely dessert served very simply with poached fruit and whipped cream. It's also a wonderful topping for sweet tarts. A word of warning: you must make sure your utensils are very clean, as a tiny trace of grease will make the meringue flop. Try not to whip it in a plastic bowl, as those can trap particles of grease – use glass or steel instead.

MAKES 6

2 egg whites
½ tsp cream of tartar
pinch of sea salt
100g caster sugar

Preheat the oven to 100°C/fan 80°C/gas mark ¼. Line a baking tray with baking parchment.

Whisk the egg whites, cream of tartar and salt using an electric whisk, gradually incorporating the caster sugar. It will become smooth and glossy, holding its shape.

Spoon the meringue into a piping bag fitted with a fluted nozzle, then pipe the meringue on to the prepared baking tray in six 9cm discs.

Bake for a good 2 hours, or until crisp and firm. Allow to cool completely on the tray before serving.

Chocolate and walnut oil pâté, orange peel muesli and walnut cream

A rich, indulgent dessert which shows a little quirkiness. It also feels a bit restauranty, so you may want to save it for when you have guests. On the other hand, you may feel as if you deserve it yourself, so go ahead. The muesli is actually crossed with a kind of crumble, so it gives a little more crunch. If you have some left over, try it with a little natural yogurt. You can have everything ready for this dessert and assemble it at the last minute, which makes you look good with minimum effort. Adding the orange zest gives a little refreshing zing. If you make the components the day before, be sure to zest an orange freshly to serve.

SERVES 6–8

150g plain flour
75g brown sugar
100g unsalted butter, chopped
100g porridge oats
sprinkle of sea salt
juice and finely grated zest of 1 orange
100g candied orange peel
450g good-quality milk chocolate, chopped

30g walnut oil
210g whipping cream, plus 100g
75g granulated sugar
50g walnuts

Preheat the oven to 180°C/fan 160°C/gas mark 4.

First things first. Put the flour, brown sugar, butter, oats and salt in a blender and pulse until you have a breadcrumb texture. Or pop it all in a bowl and rub with your fingers until the breadcrumb texture is reached, just like in the old days.

Next pulse or mix in the orange juice; it will go a bit sticky but don't worry. Don't over-mix; stop as soon as it is mixed, because you don't want a ball of pastry.

Take a tray lined with greaseproof paper and spread out the mix, trying to break it up as we are looking for a crumbled result.

Bake for 20–25 minutes or until golden brown, turning every 5 minutes with a spatula so that the mix cooks evenly. Allow to cool, then break up into muesli-looking pieces and fold in the candied orange peel. Store in an airtight container for up to 3 days.

This is the easiest part. Put the chocolate in a good-sized bowl, then in a saucepan bring the walnut oil and the 210g of cream to a boil. Pour this on to the chocolate and stir until it is thoroughly melted and combined. You can store this in an airtight container until needed; it will keep for 3 days in the fridge.

This is the hardest part. First of all, place a piece of greaseproof paper on the worktop, about 30cm long should do. Now take a frying pan and sprinkle the granulated sugar over it in an even layer. Place over a gentle heat and allow to melt, but do not stir.

Watch the sugar carefully, as it will turn quickly. When it starts to become a golden caramel colour, stir in the walnuts. Be careful, it is hot. As soon as they are coated in the caramel, remove from the heat and turn out on to the paper. Allow to cool; 10 minutes should be enough. Well done, you have made praline. When cooled, place the nuts in a bowl and hit with the end of a rolling pin to smash them up a bit. In an airtight container, they will keep until the next day, but no longer or they will go soft. (Make sure the container is airtight.)

When you are ready to serve, simply whip the 100g of cream until it forms soft peaks and carefully fold in the walnut praline.

To serve, take a bowl and add a couple of spoonfuls of muesli. Then use an ice-cream scoop that has been dipped in a little warm water to scoop a ball of chocolate on to the muesli. Add a spoon of the walnut cream and finally sprinkle on the orange zest.

Lemon and lime meringue with coconut crumble

This is one of those dishes which make you look really smart, but is actually really easy to make. Lemon, lime and coconut are good friends and this is an interesting way to present them. The dish is assembled at the last minute so that, when your guests jump in, it is still nice and crisp. The recipe calls for Lemon curd (see page 113) but don't bother making it just for this recipe, you are welcome to use some from the shop (just make sure it's decent).

SERVES 6

1 quantity of Meringue, unbaked (see page 207)

150g plain flour
115g caster sugar
35g unsalted butter
30g desiccated coconut
65g coconut oil
1 lime
12 tbsp lemon curd, preferably home-made (see page 113)

finely grated zest of 1 unwaxed lemon or lime

Follow the recipe for the meringue, making sure that all your equipment is clean and that you add the sugar gradually. When it has become smooth and glossy, put it into a piping bag fitted with a star nozzle.

Take a piece of baking parchment and a cutter which is 8cm in diameter – or thereabouts – and, using the cutter as a template, draw six circles on the parchment with a pencil, making sure you leave a couple of centimetres between them. Now turn the paper over; you should be able to see the circles on the other side.

Using the circles as a guide, pipe peaks of meringue about 2cm high around the circles, making sure each peak touches the next. Continue like this in ever-decreasing concentric rings until the circle is full of peaks which are touching.

Place in the oven and cook as directed on page 113. When cooked and cooled, store the meringues in an airtight box until needed, for up to 1 day (pop them back in the oven for 10 minutes on a low heat if they go soft).

For the crumble, preheat the oven to 180°C/fan 160°C/gas mark 4. Put the flour, sugar, butter, coconut and coconut oil in a blender and pulse until it is well mixed but still crumbly. Place a piece of baking parchment on a baking tray and tip on the crumble mix. Push it together to make a mass, but don't compact it too hard, as it needs to be crumbly. Place the 8cm cutter over the top to check it will be big enough for six circles.

Bake for 10 minutes, then remove from the oven and use the cutter to make preliminary circles (it is easier to get sharp circles when part-cooked than when fully cooked). Return to the oven and cook for another 20–25 minutes or until golden.

Remove the crumble from the oven and, using your cutter, just go over the circles again to make sure they will come apart later. Leave on the tray until completely cooled, then, using a palette knife, carefully remove the six circles and keep in an airtight box until you are ready, or for up to 3 days. You can eat the scraps – that's a little treat.

Use a grater to finely grate the zest from the lime into a bowl, then slice the lime in half and squeeze the juice into the bowl. Mix in the lemon curd; this is now your lemon and lime curd.

To serve, take a small amount of lemon curd mixture, about the size of your fingernail, and place in the middle of a plate. Put a coconut crumble on top of this (the lemon curd is the glue sticking the crumble to the plate, you see). Do this for the rest of the crumbles; be careful, they are fragile.

Next divide the lemon and lime curd between the crumbles and smooth down with a knife, making sure you push right to the edge. Now top each with a meringue crown. You may notice that the crown is about the same size as the crumble base, so it looks nice and neat.

Sprinkle with the lemon or lime zest, allowing some to fall on to the plate, then serve. If you wish, add a spoon of whipped cream.

Peanut butter cheesecake with salted toffee sauce

A very bad dessert, almost an overload of naughtiness, if there is such a thing. We have included cocoa nibs, which are roasted cacao beans; they are quite bitter, yet have a deep chocolate flavour that helps to give the base an intriguing taste. As there is no baking involved and we do not use gelatine, this cheesecake relies on the chilling process to set it. You will probably have too much toffee sauce, but I'm sure you will find something to do with any leftovers. You can also make a dairy-free version of this cheesecake using vegan cream cheese, but make sure you buy a good-quality version, as some of them can turn quite slack when mixed.

SERVES 6–8

50g unsalted butter, melted (or dairy-free margarine), plus more for the tin

100g digestive biscuits (if making a dairy-free version, check the label)

20g cocoa nibs, plus more to serve (optional)

250g full fat cream cheese, or good-quality vegan cream cheese (low-fat versions won't work)

80g whipping cream (or soy cream for the dairy-free)

30g icing sugar
300g crunchy peanut butter
1 quantity Salted butterscotch (see page 117), or vegan toffee sauce

Butter a 20cm diameter loose-bottomed tin, then line it with baking parchment.

Place the biscuits in a plastic bag and hit them with something heavy such as a rolling pin or a pan. Place the crumbs in a bowl with the melted butter and cocoa nibs, mix, then press into the tin, making sure all the edges are straight. Place in the fridge so it can set while you make the filling.

Put the cream cheese, cream and icing sugar in a food mixer and beat for a minute to combine, or use a spoon and a bowl. When completely combined, carefully fold in the peanut butter but do not mix it in thoroughly; you want to create a rippled effect.

Spoon the mix on to the base and, using a metal spoon (a wooden one tends to drag the cheese), flatten and smooth so it is flat and even. Place in the fridge for 2 hours to firm up; this should be sufficient, but fridge temperatures do differ.

After 2 hours in the fridge, push a sharp knife into the middle – if it feels like a cheesecake it is set; if not, pop it in the freezer for 10 minutes, but don't forget about it.

To serve, carefully remove from the tin, slice into wedges, and serve with Salted butterscotch. Or spread a spoonful of butterscotch on a plate, sprinkle with a few cocoa nibs and add a cheesecake wedge on top. Very pretty.

Baked pineapple with crispy rice and roasted white chocolate

This is an amazing dessert; however, with this recipe you are entering a chef's world: using caramel and roasting white chocolate. Those of you who have worked with chocolate before will know that it does not like extreme heat. However, the results are quite interesting, so get stuck in. A little advice: buy yourself some really good baking parchment – that cheap stuff just will not do. Interesting information: pineapples do not ripen once they are cut from the plant, they just rot, so if a pineapple is under-ripe when you buy it, that's how it will stay.

SERVES 6

600g good-quality white chocolate
1 ripe pineapple
50g demerara sugar
120g granulated sugar
good pinch of sea salt
80g popped rice cereal – that's right, breakfast cereal

20g unsalted butter

Let's do the technical bit first. Preheat the oven to 150°C/fan 130°C/gas mark 2, no more, no less. Chop the chocolate with a sharp knife; don't be too particular, it's going to melt anyway. Place good-quality baking parchment on a baking tray, then add the chocolate. Spread it around so it is in an even layer, but keep it close together, you don't want stray pieces because they burn.

Set a timer for 10 minutes, then place the chocolate on the middle shelf. At 10 minutes remove from the oven, stir, then pop back in for two minutes. Remove and cool. When cold, chop roughly and store in an airtight container for up to 4 days.

Increase the oven temperature to 220°C/fan 200°C/gas mark 7. Slice off the top and bottom of the pineapple, stand it upright and, from the top to the bottom, slice off the skin. Then, using a sharp knife, hold the pineapple in your hand and slice 'V' shapes along the lines of the eyes to remove them. Stand the pineapple upright and cut it in half, then cut each half into three wedges and slice off the core (the firmer bit on the sharp side). Well done.

Put the wedges in a high-sided tin. Sprinkle with the demerara sugar, then bake for 15 minutes, turning once to coat in the sugar. Remove and allow to cool.

Finally the rice. Place a strip of good baking parchment on a work top as you will not have time later – about 50cm long should do. Using the largest frying pan you have, add 40g of water, the granulated sugar and salt and bring to a simmer. Do not stir, otherwise you run the risk of crystallising the sugar.

When the sugar is just beginning to colour at the edges, add the popped rice cereal and stir constantly until the pieces are a golden brown. Be careful, this will be very hot.

Remove from the heat, then fold in the butter until melted and immediately turn out on to the baking parchment, flattening it out a little to help it to cool, then leave to completely cool and set. When set, smash with a rolling pin. Be careful though, you don't want it all over the kitchen and you want to keep some texture and some shards. Store in an airtight container until needed, or for up to 4 days.

To serve, carve the pineapple wedges into thin slices, add a line of white chocolate crumbles along the plate and top with the pineapple, then sprinkle on the crispy rice. This should be enough but, if you wish, add a scoop of vanilla ice cream... better still, white chocolate ice cream, if you can find some.

Acknowledgements

This is the bit where we say thanks to all the usual and unusual suspects. Here goes.

Thanks to parents and family for all the usual reasons, especially George for painting and decorating with us. Friends, you know who you are, thanks to you also.

In memory of our Nanna Joyce who made us feel very special when, despite being unwell visited us in our little York restaurant, and was so proud of us.

A huge thanks to staff, past, present and future; without you this page would not exist. And to everyone who has dined with us over the years and continually supported us.

Thank you, Victoria Hobbs, for finding us and showing us how to go about this whole book thing.

Of course we cannot forget to mention the people at Saltyard – Elizabeth, Kate, Lucy, Laura and Rosie and all the rest of the team. Well done for guiding us through.

A big thanks to Alice, who co-wrote the recipes and used to be a chef at Vanilla Black.

There's others: Michelle Jackson for telling people all those years ago that we existed. Kevin Connolly for too many things to list. Vicki Havron, who still maintains that she was our first member of staff (?) and Nanna Rose (she's not really our Nanna) for laundering the tea towels. Nathan Wogman (had to name drop someone famous) for the guided tours of London.

ISBN 978 1 444 79400 7
eBook ISBN 978 1 444 79401 4

Book design by Cabin London
Typeset in Sabon

Copy editor Lucy Bannell
Proof reader Annie Lee
Indexer Caroline Wilding
Food stylist Alice Hart
Props stylist Lucy Attwater

Printed and bound in China by
C&C Offset Printing Co., Ltd.

Hodder & Stoughton policy is to use
papers that are natural, renewable and
recyclable products and made from wood
grown in sustainable forests. The logging
and manufacturing processes are expected
to conform to the environmental
regulations of the country of origin.

Saltyard Books
Carmelite House
50 Victoria Embankment
London EC4Y 0DZ

www.saltyardbooks.co.uk

First published in Great Britain in 2015
by Saltyard Books
An imprint of Hodder & Stoughton
An Hachette UK company

1

Copyright © Andrew Dargue 2015
Photography © Emma Lee 2015

The right of Andrew Dargue to be identified as
the Author of the Work has been asserted by
him in accordance with the Copyright, Designs
and Patents Act 1988.

All rights reserved. No part of this
publication may be reproduced, stored
in a retrieval system, or transmitted, in
any form or by any means without the
prior written permission of the publisher,
nor be otherwise circulated in any form
of binding or cover other than that in
which it is published and without a
similar condition being imposed on the
subsequent purchaser.

A CIP catalogue record for this title
is available from the British Library.